DISCOV
AMBER ᴠᴀʟʟᴇʏ

Sailing boats on Ogston Reservoir

TEN WALKS THAT REVEAL THE
HISTORY OF OGSTON RESERVOIR
AND THE SURROUNDING AREA

JILL ARMITAGE

COUNTRY BOOKS

Published by Country Books/Ashridge Press
Courtyard Cottage, Little Longstone, Bakewell, Derbyshire DE45 1NN
Tel: 01629 640670
e-mail: dickrichardson@country-books.co.uk

ISBN 978-1-906789-11-4

© 2009 Jill Armitage

ACKNOWLEDGEMENT

After fifty-five years, many people still remember the pre-reservoir days with a nostalgic fondness. It is to them that I would like to dedicate this book to express my appreciation for sharing their memories and making this book possible.

My sincere thanks go to Mr Burt Hopkinson, an expert on the area and one of the Ogston farmers who lost over half his land; Mr Sam Fox whose ancestors have lived and worked in Woolley for countless generations; Mr Gladwyn Turbutt whose family owned and worked the Ogston estate, and Mrs Elisabeth Bowden who lived at Woolley camp throughout the war years. For their visual contributions I am particularly indebted to Mrs Elisabeth Bowden, Mrs Jan Rogers and Mr Geoff Lumb. No amount of research would be possible without dedicated library staff so to the girls of Clay Cross library and Matlock Local Studies, particularly the three Sues, thank you. And last but not least many thanks to David Melville who started the hare.

Printed and bound in England by Digital Book Print Ltd.
Tel: 01908 733084

INTRODUCTION

Look westward across the valley from the A61 between Stretton and Higham, the old Roman Road named Rykneld Street, and you are faced with a most impressive panorama. Deep in this peaceful, secluded valley lies a reservoir nestling in a bowl of green countryside that rises gently on all sides.

Over the centuries, the busy world passed by and few gave a glance down into this picturesque valley with its timeless tranquillity. Then the railways came, opencast mining, a light railway and a 210 acre reservoir. Each of these intrusions left scars that have healed with time, but the latter effectively destroyed the economic viability of three estate farms and a picturesque Derbyshire hamlet with its cottages, mill, ancient alehouse and mansion.

'The innate character of the valley as it existed for hundreds of years is now irrevocably lost,' said Gladwin Turbutt of Ogston Hall as the rising waters of the new Ogston reservoir engulfed the valley.

With the passage of time its inevitable that changes occur and landscapes mature but overall this is an area unscathed by human intervention. Even the reservoir which changed the valley for ever is now a focal point of outstanding beauty.

Discover the Amber Valley tells the story of the coming of the reservoir and the history of an area rich in history, heritage and charm. We can lament the destruction of the hamlet of Woolley while at the same time, rejoicing in the discovering of what we still have through a collection of walks that are all circular in route and centralised around the reservoir.

Through a combination of quiet lanes, pastoral paths, old turnpike roads and original pack-horse trails chosen for their scenic value and interest, these ancient routes give us a spider's web of wonderful walks.

Several paths pass through or very close to domestic premises because the original intention of such footpaths was to provide the most direct route for these remote occupants to reach chapel, shops or transportation links. Many of these buildings are still working farms so please show consideration particularly when walking through farm yards and in summer when fields are often full of crops or cattle.

Respect, protect and most of all, enjoy the Amber Valley.

It's a fascinating place and it has never looked more beautiful.

Jill Armitage 2009

Note: Bold numbers in the walks refer to the further information beginning on page 77

CONTENTS

WALKS 1-10

FURTHER INFORMATION

1: OGSTON CIRCULAR ROUTE
Walk: Just over 4 miles – 6·6km

An opportunity to walk all the way round Ogston Reservoir combining a blend of quiet lanes, a pastoral path beside the River Amber, a mile long reservoir promenade and an old turnpike road.
Pass through the isolated hamlet of Ford, over the track of the Ashover Light Railway, through Brackenfield; discover a bird-hide, and the lost hamlet of Woolley Bridge.

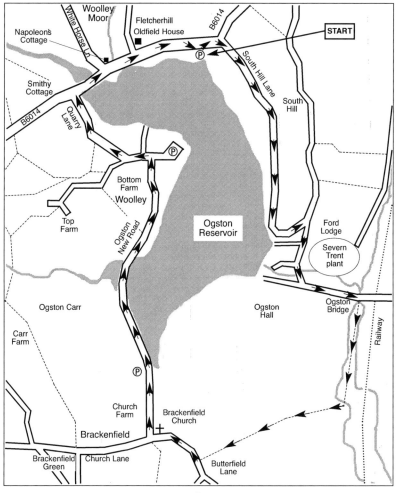

This walk starts from the car park north of Ogston Reservoir (**1**) situated on the B6014, two miles South West of Stretton. Originally, this was an old turn-pike road (**2**) from Matlock to Mansfield.

The car park is on the site of Mill Lane (**3**) which led down into the valley to serve Woolley Mill (**4**).

✱ Leave the car park onto the B6014 and turn right up the hill.

✱ In 150 metres, turn right into a narrow road flanked by 'No Through Road' signs. This is South Hill Lane.

South Hill Lane

View over the reservoir from South Hill Lane

✱ Follow this road which runs along eastern boundary of the reservoir. The hillside between is wooded but there are some tantalising glimpses of the reservoir.

After 1,000 metres, the head of the dam (**5**) is reached. This is where, pre-reservoir days, South Hill would have been joined from across the valley by

Hurst Lane. Through the trees behind the dam is the outline of Ogston Hall (6) the former home of the Turbutt family.

✱ Continue along this road which is now Hurst Lane and the main thoroughfare to the tiny hamlet of Ford. A high curving wall on your right is the boundary of the former Ford House and Ford Old House (7), both demolished when the dam was constructed.

✱ Follow the road round to your right, past Ford Lodge on your left and continue straight ahead. The route now passes through part of the Severn Trent Water Authority's Treatment Plant.

This is the old Ford Lane, a bridleway connecting Ford with Ogston, and where the River Amber originally forded giving the hamlet its name. Later, due to flooding, the lane was raised considerably and a stone, arch bridge provided.

Ford Lane and the bridge over the River Amber where the river used to 'ford'

A section of raised embankment over to your left is the only evidence in this area of the existence of the Ashover Light Railway (8) which passed straight through here en route to Ashover. Having left its parallel course with the main railway line on a gradually falling gradient, the ALR reached its lowest point at Ford.

During construction of the

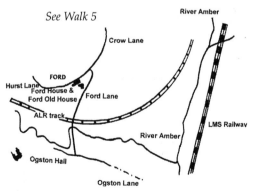

Ford, showing the river, road and railway routes pre-reservoir construction

9

railway track, it was necessary to straighten the watercourse of the River Amber here to avoid the need to provide two railway bridges. A short siding was provided to accommodate two wagons of coal delivered regularly for Ogston Hall (6).

Since its closure in the 1950's the route of the ALR has become a private service road for Severn Trent Water Authority personnel to Smithy Moor on the South side of the B6014. It is known locally as Peggy Lane, because a favourite name for the narrow gauge railway was the 'Peggy Line', named after 'Peggy', one of the engines.

✱ Continue until you reach the rear entrance gates of Ogston Hall (6) which are on your right, veer to your left into Ogston Lane, the old bridle road that leads to Higham (9).

Back entrance gate to Ogston Hall

Ogston Lane with Higham Hillside in the background

Ogston Lane has always been a private carriage-way for Ogston Hall. However, Mary Holland of Ford House, sister of Elizabeth Turbutt of Ogston Hall also used this private road. For the privilege she paid her sister one penny, but the turnpike trust saw this as a means of avoiding tolls and the Commissioner of the Tibshelf and Matlock Turnpike road complained that by using this road, the people of Ford were defrauding Smithy Moor Toll Bar.

Richard Turbutt agreed, stating that anyone using Ogston Lane and not going to Ogston should be made to pay.

* Proceed along Ogston Lane with Higham Hillside (**10**) ahead. All this land was once part of the Ogston estate.

> **Note**: To continue **Walk One,** the route from here is no longer suitable for wheelchair users.

* Where the Ogston Lane crosses the River Amber, go down steps on the far side of the river, turn right and and follow its meanderings through water meadows. The river should be on your right, the railway cutting on your left along this stretch. **Walk Eight B** which begins at The Greyhound Hotel at Higham will join **Walk One** here.

* Cross an iron footbridge, then stay with the river to its first bend. Go straight ahead to a stile beside an oak tree. Continue across the middle of the next field.

* Cross a stile that gives access to an ancient lane between sparse hedges. The path ends at a six bar gate by which is a wooden stile and half hidden in the hedge is a rusty 'footpath' sign.

You are now on a tarmac road picturesquely named Butterfield Lane. Opposite is Tanyard Farm which in the 19th century was the Brackenfield Tannery.

The wooden stile by
the gate on Butterfield Lane

11

Butterfield Lane

✱ Turn right and continue past a couple of farms and the Brackenfield village sign (11) until reaching Brackenfield Church (11B).

Looking through the lych gate of Brackenfield Church

The view towards Ogston Reservoir from Brackenfield churchyard

✱ Turn right along Ogston New Road (**13**) signposted to Woolley (**14**).

In 1847, a 'new road' was made between Woolley and Brackenfield, enabling a new, shorter carriage-way to be constructed in place of the old precipitous bridleway known as 'Rocky Road' between Ogston and Brackenfield. This 'new road' is now the old road and there is an obvious seam between the wider, straighter stretch of the Ogston New Road and the old road at both ends. This is much narrower and without any form of footpath so take care!

✱ Pass Ogston Lodge (**12**) on your left and the drive entrance to Ogston Hall (**6**) on your right. Both needed re-siting with the coming of the reservoir.

The entrance to Ogston Hall

Ogston Lodge

Here on your left is a car park. If the circular walk is too strenuous or for wheelchair/buggy users, start the walk here, although you will have to retrace your steps.

✳ Continue along this road which now skirts the water's edge. The profuse band of marginal trees and shrubs planted round the reservoir in the 1960's almost obscures the view in places.

The boundary wall along this stretch of road was built with the stone reclaimed from the buildings demolished when the reservoir was built. Even though it was cut-stone and quite unsuitable for dry stone-walling, Mr Jackson was the builder and guys from Sheffield built these walls at piece rate. They had no idea how to dry stone wall and the walls fell down very quickly, but Mr Bowler and Mr Robertson of Ashover Hay were good. Their walls are still standing almost sixty years later.

Cut stone from the demolished properties was used for the 'dry stone walling' along this stretch of the reservoir

Pause to admire the view across the valley and try to imagine what is was like when it was all quiet fields with a meandering river and the Ashover Light Railway (**8**) chugging along between Ford and Woolley Bridge (**25**).

Boats on Ogston Reservoir

✱ When the footpath peters out, the stone walling ends and the road narrows, you are entering the old stretch of road. A little further, where the road bends to your left, note the attractive building. This is Bottom Farm, Woolley but originally this area was known as Oxon (15). When the reservoir came, Bottom Farm lost all of its eighty one acres.

Bottom Farm

✱ At the bend, take a detour to the right into the car-park. This was the site of the old Hurst Lane which continued across the valley, crossing the River Amber at Hurst Bridge and on to Ford. In the far corner of the car park is the stone 'hide' of the Ogston Bird Club, previously the Ogston Hide Group (16).
✱ Leave the car park. Proceed up Hurst Lane and pass the entrance to the Sailing Club (17). This was originally the site of the Amber Valley Camp (18).

Some wit has defaced the sign which should read 'private fishing'

The entrance to Ogston Sailing Club. The building in the background, now used as a club house was originally built for the use of the Amber Valley Camp

✳ Pause to look through the gates as this was the start of Mill Lane which during the time of the camp's existence passed through the centre and ran across the valley to Woolley Mill (4). The building which you can see and now serves as the club house was originally the cafeteria of the Amber Valley Camp School.

On the opposite side of the road is a long barn where Bottom Farm's bull used to be housed. It's now a rather smart holiday cottage.

✳ Go up this road until it veers to the right. If you look straight ahead you will see a small settlement of farms (19). These were the ones hit worst by the building of the reservoir.

✳ Follow the road as it bends to the right. It becomes Quarry Lane due to the sandstone quarries on both sides of the road. They are now disused. Stone quarried here would have been taken down Mill Lane to be cut and polished at the mill. The stone was used to build and decorate many local properties including the new frontage to Ogston Hall (6) in the early 1850's.

✳ Continue along Quarry Lane.

The newly refurbished building on the left was originally Woolley Primitive Methodist Chapel (20). The construction of the reservoir didn't effect the chapel but it had fallen into a bad state of repair. It was sold in 2002 with a site of approximately two acres and planning consent for conversion to a two storey dwelling and a further single storey extension. Now completed, it is a fine private residence.

*The old Methodist chapel conversion with Draycott's Holdings
(now Old Farm) in the background*

Almost opposite the old chapel was a narrow lane that led to a couple of cottages, now demolished, and on your left is another recent rebuild. Originally Draycott's Holdings (21) it is now a private residence called Old Farm.

16

✱ Proceed to the road junction of the B6014. This used to be a cross roads as directly opposite Quarry Lane was Sheffield Street (**22**). The only surviving building here now is Smithy Cottage (**23**) which sixty/seventy years ago was 'Ma Young's Tea Room'.

Smithy Cottage, once 'Ma Youngs' Tea Room

✱ Turn right and proceed down the hill. This stretch of road is known as Dark Lane (**24**). Originally there were a number of properties along here including a toll bar cottage on the Mansfield/Matlock Turnpike Road.

✱ As you reach the lowest point of the road, this is where the road bridge crossed the River Amber and traditionally where Woolley and Woolley Moor meet. The area to the west of the River Amber is Woolley, the area on the east bank is Woolley Moor.

Floods were recorded in 1825 when the dam at Bump Mill, Kelstedge burst its banks. It destroyed bridges over the Amber as far downstream as Woolley, where the bridge was washed away and had to be rebuilt. One hundred and thirty years later, this stretch of road had to be raised considerably to bring it above top water-level when the reservoir was built.

Dark Lane had to be raised to bring it above the water level

17

Between 1925-50, the Ashover Light Railway crossed the B6014 here (**25**), at a gated crossing, one of only two on the line. By the side of the railway line on the opposite side of the road, was Amber House (**26**).

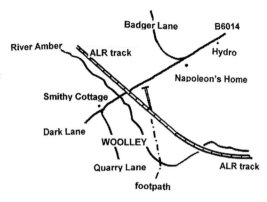

Woolley Bridge area, showing the river, road and railway routes

Ironically, ALR Woolley station and siding were situated on the east of the river, so the station was actually Woolley Moor not Woolley. This is also where Mr Harold Fox parked his bus (**27**) and where the bus service to Stretton station and Clay Cross ran from.

The ALR siding actually bordered the stone wall of the orchard of Napoleons Home (**28**). Both the bus service and the inn were owned and run by the Fox family as was the village petrol pump situated in front of a stone barn next door. The petrol supply was tanked in the orchard behind.

✱ Continue along Dark Lane, skirting the reservoir and enjoy the views. On the end of Badger Lane (also known as White Horse Lane) is Napoleon's Cottage. Edgar Fox lived in Napoleon's Cottage and fearing this might be pulled down too, bought Oldfield House, situated further up the road at the junction of Temperance Hill. Fortunately his fears were unfounded and the cottage remains.

Napoleon's Cottage

18

✱ Carry on along Dark Lane as the road begins to rise gradually. Here on your right was Woolley House/Hydro (**29**), that had been converted into separate dwellings and a shop after its use as a Hydropathic establishment had ceased. Although not inundated this building was considered too near to the water line to be saved.

✱ Pass the junction to Temperance Hill where the first Woolley Show (**32**) was held in the damson orchard in 1911. Damson juice was commonly used to dye stockings made locally in the days before synthetic dyes were invented.

✱ Continue along Dark Lane and on the opposite side of the road just past the junction of Temperance Hill (also known as Fletcher Hill) is Oldfield House which after the closure of Napoleon's Home became the New Napoleon. Owned by the Fox family, it was in a field by the side of the New Napoleon that Mr Fox discarded his old bus when the service had ceased (**27**). The New Napoleon is now a private house.

Oldfield House became the New Napoleon public house
but is now once again a private residence

✱ Go past Oldfield House, up the hill and the car park which is the start/end of the wallk is on your right.

2: WOOLLEY MOOR
Walk: 1⅓ miles – just over 2km

An enjoyable short stroll on quiet country lanes. The walk incorporates an old coaching inn, the hamlet of Badger Lane and the lost hamlet of Woolley Bridge that disappeared under the reservoir. With slight variations this short walk is suitable for wheelchair/buggy users and helpers with stamina.

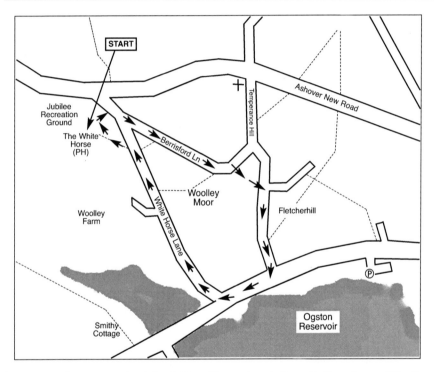

* Begin at the Car Park of the White Horse Inn (**31**) on Badger Lane, Woolley Moor. Go to the bottom right hand corner of the car park. Here you will find an entrance into the Jubilee Recreation Ground where the annual Woolley Show (**32**) is held.

Note: Wheelchair users may prefer to leave the car-park at the entrance into Badger Lane cross the road and take the path between the houses opposite. This will bring you out on Beresford Lane.

The old sign showing a white horse pulling a cart loaded with a 'badger' of salt

✱ Enjoy the enchanting view. Across the top of the hills opposite is Coffin Road which is the old route taken by coffin bearers from the neighbouring hamlets of Lea and Dethick to Ashover. These settlements were without their own burial grounds, so corpses were brought to the mother church at Ashover for their religious interment. Walk Nine walks along the Coffin Road.
✱ Proceed through the recreation ground and leave via a narrow road between the houses near to the children's play ground through to the road. This area was originally a hamlet called Badger Lane (**34**) and pre-1840 consisted of just five dwellings which included the Toll Bar Cottage at the end of this road, the three cottages on your right and the White Horse Inn.
✱ Turn right down the road and walk past those earliest three cottages.

The three cottages that formed the hamlet of Badger Lane

21

The house on the corner, Perkins Cottage, was formerly a shop. The extension on the side provided the extra space for a post office, and the owner Joe Spencer also ran a delivery service and sold paraffin. The shop was always packed and goods were stacked up the stairs. When the Waldrons took over the business, they built a new post office opposite the old cottages. When this closed the building became a private house which was named Post House.

✱ Cross Badger Lane (also known as White Horse Lane) and proceed down Berrisford Lane.

The Chesterfield Rural District Council built eighteen new council houses and bungalows here to provide nearby alternative housing for the people of Woolley and Woolley Moor who had lost their homes with the commencement of the reservoir.

> **Note**: Wheelchair users who left the White Horse Inn at the Badger Lane entrance and took the path between the houses opposite will join at this point.

✱ On your left is Stretton Handley Church of England Primary School built in 1969.

Continue down Beresford Lane until you reach Linacre House on your left. Almost opposite on your right is a narrow path which tends to get rather overgrown. This is Well Lane.

> **Note**: For wheelchair users, continue down Beresford Lane, and at the bottom of the road is a stone bridge. Keep to your right and turn right into Temperance Hill. Join the route at an area of grassland on your right.

✱ On Well Lane, walk down the stone edged steps. These are the sign of an old track.

The stone edgedsteps on Well Lane

22

✱ In the dip at the bottom you will see a stream which starts in Littlemoor and flows into Ogston Reservoir. There was a well here, thus the name, where the residents of Woolley House Hydro (29) and the cottages on Temperance Hill got their water. The water here is said to be so clear that freshwater shrimps can be found.

✱ Cross the stream by the narrow foot-bridge, climb up the far bank and you will be on Temperance Hill. This little hamlet was originally known as Fletcher Hill and locals also refer to it as Woolley Hillocks.

If you want a hundred yard detour to your left, Temperance Hill joins the Ashover New Road at cross-roads with Handley. Here is St. Mark's School and Church. The foundation stone was laid in April 1869 and the building costs were £317.1s 6d. The school opened in April 1870, a year before Foster's Elementary Education Act made schooling compulsory.

If you haven't taken a look at St Mark's church, turn right and on your right are Temperance Hill Cottages.

Mrs Cowlishawe who lived in one of these cottages used to have a small shop in the front room. These were known as parlour shops. At the rear of the last two cottages is a small brick building originally a stocking factory. Before artificially derived alternatives became readily available, natural dyes were used to dye the finished stockings so the area next to the stocking factory was well stocked with damson trees for this purpose. The first Woolley Show (32) was held in this damson orchard.

✱ Continue down the hill towards Ogston reservoir (1). The building on the left at the back of Oldfield House is now residential and called Oldfield Barn. At the bottom of the hill is the junction with the main B6014, the original Mansfield/Matlock turnpike road (2).

✱ To continue walk two, turn right and proceed along Dark Lane (24). The road now skirts the water's edge and pre-reservoir days, this area would have been a hub of activity. The land by the side of the reservoir was where the Woolley House/Hydro (29) stood. Further along, The Ashover Light Railway (25) crossed the main road here, the ALR station was here, the village petrol pump was positioned here, Fox's transport (27) left from here, and here stood Napoleons Home (28), the ancient ale house. Now all that is left is Napoleon's Cottage on your left.

✱ Just past Napoleon's Cottage, turn right into Badger Lane, also known as White Horse Lane. This is the most strenuous stage of the journey with the road climbing gradually all the way. Pass Woolley Farm in the dip on your left and almost at the top of the lane is The White Horse Inn on your left, and the start/end of the walk.

Looking down Temperance Hill towards the reservoir

IF YOU WOULD LIKE TO COMBINE WALKS ONE AND TWO, TURN LEFT ONTO THE B6014. PASS OLDFIELD HOUSE AND PROCEED UP THE HILL UNTIL YOU REACH THE CAR PARK ON YOUR RIGHT, NORTH OF THE RESERVOIR.

3: OGSTON – HANDLEY – DALEBANK
Walk: 5 miles – 8km

A walk that allows you to look down over Ogston reservoir from the neighbouring hamlet of Handley. With views over Clay Cross, you will also see one of the oldest properties in the area dating from 1590, a toll bar cottage, a thatched cottage, and part of the route of the ALR from Dalebank to Woolley.

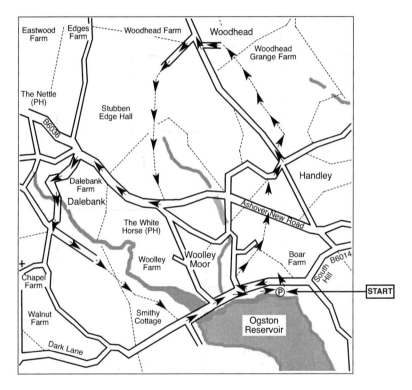

This walk begins at the car park north of Ogston Reservoir (1) situated on the B6014, two miles south west of Stretton. Originally this was an old turnpike road (2) from Mansfield to Matlock.

Before you begin your walk look across the reservoir and imagine what this area was like pre-reservoir days. The site of the sailing club on the opposite bank was Amber Valley Camp School and from your vantage point in the car park, Mill Lane (3) ran down the valley to serve Woolley Mill (4), then up past the camp to join Quarry Lane.

Before leaving the car park look across the reservoir to the sailing club on the far bank. This was originally Amber Valley Camp

✱ Leave the car park onto the B6014 and turn left down the hill. Immediately after passing the New Napoleon which is now a private house renamed Oldfield House on your right, turn right up Fletcher Hill (also known as Temperance Hill) leaving Ogston Reservoir (1) behind you.

At the end of the garden of Oldfield Barn on your right is a stone stile in the hedge.

The stone stile in the hedge on Temperance Hill

The stile on Ashover New Road

✱ Pass through the stile and head diagonally across the next three fields and out onto the farm track to Handley Field Farm. This is one of the oldest properties in the area and apparently got its name because the original owner could only afford to buy one field. The track continues next to the farm so look for the date stone 1590 on the farmhouse. Walk straight ahead until the path comes out on the B6036.

✱ Look to your left where you will see a cross-roads at the end of Temperance Hill with Handley Lane. Here is St. Mark's School and Church which was completed in 1870. Cross the road to the stile on the other side. Walk up the field to the top left corner to meet the road. After climbing over this stile, turn and look at the view.

The view from Handley with Handley Field Farm and Ogston

The stile on Handley Lane

27

✱ Walk up the hill to Handley where you will pass Handley Mission Church dated 1874 on your right. The establishment of a church at Handley coincided with a period of great Christian zeal and energy which saw the building of many small churches and chapels promoted with vigour. We have just encountered St Mark's School and Church at the crossroads at Woolley Moor which was completed in 1840. On Walk One we pass the Primitive Methodist Chapel on Quarry Lane, also built in 1840 and Brackenfield church in 1856. In the distance on the next stretch of this walk we can see Clay Cross church which was consecrated on January 25th 1851.

The building of Handley Mission Church is credited to the efforts of the Reverend Joseph Oldham of North Wingfield parish who opened a subscription list headed by His Grace the Duke of Devonshire, resident of Chatsworth House. Gladwin Turbutt of Ogston Hall gave the site and building was completed in 1874 according to the date stone under the arched window in the south westerly facing wall. Its interesting to read the stone plaque which refers to it as the new CONNEXION CHAPEL – the three Ns in connection are backward and its spelt with X.

Handley Chapel and the window with the dedication stone below

From correspondence in 1926 with the diocesan authorities, apparently there was some concern that Handley Mission Church had not been licensed for worship, despite it being in operation for 56 years. In order to rectify that, the church was licensed immediately, just to be sure.

✱ Turn left into Woodhead Lane. After a short distance, you will see a footpath sign by a gap in the hedge.

Stubben Edge Hall

✱ Walk across the field to the right corner. Walk through a stone stile through a gap in the hedge. Cross to the next stile and pause to enjoy the view over the fields and the environs of Clay Cross which pre-1841 was no more than a village.

When George Stephenson was constructing the North Midland Railway between Derby and Leeds, he built a tunnel under what is now Clay Cross and having discovered coal, formed The Clay Cross Company to extract and market it. George Stephenson and his son Robert were in partnership, then Sir William Jackson Bart., M.P – Chairman from 1862-1876, the first of five generations of the Jackson family who held control of the Clay Cross Company for over 100 years. It was Brigadier General Jackson – Director of the company from 1891 and Chairman 1930-1946 – who formed the Ashover Light Railway (8) which ran from the company's headquarters at Egstow, Clay Cross to Ashover.

✱ Keep to the boundary fence of this downward sloping field and follow the outer edge of the next field. Walk down until a stone-pillared stile is reached. Cross over the stile and keep to the boundary edge again. Walk up the track and walk through a stone-pillared stile into a field. Walk to the side of the property ahead – Woodhead Grange Farm – and after crossing the next stile, follow a surfaced track onto Woodhead Lane.

The path comes out by the side of a dormer-bungalow named The Limes.

✱ Turn right, then left into Woodhead Farm. Keep to the track which passes

29

between the farm house and buildings.

✱ Follow the descending track from the farm and at the forked junction take the left branch towards Woolley Moor. Cross this field heading for a small copse. Cross over the brook before crossing the stile ahead and climb up the bank. Follow the well-trodden narrow path across the next field boundary to the top right hand corner where there is a stile.

Over on your right amongst the trees, Stubben Edge Hall (37), can just be seen. This was previously the home of Mr John Peter Jackson, Managing Director of the Clay Cross Company – 1876-1899. In 1962 it was purchased by Major David Kenning whose grandfather started the Kenning Motor Group, another hugely successful company based in Clay Cross.

✱ Aim for the bottom right hand corner of the next field where there is a stile and the perimeter of the garden centre. Keep to the field boundary on your right.

✱ Cross a ditch and bear left at a stile keeping to the field boundary to a stile near the left hand corner of Riley's Chrysanthemums on the B6036, Ashover New Road. When you reach the road, turn right. This is the end of Ashover New Road which at the Toll Bar Cottage (33) on your left merges into Badger Lane (34).

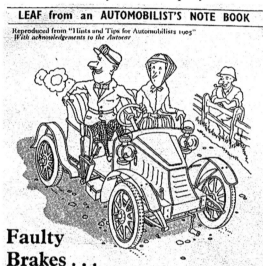
A rather humourous 1903 advertisement for the Kenning Motor Group of Clay Cross

Toll Bar Cottage

Walk along this beech-lined section of Badger Lane that runs away from Woolley Moor until reaching Stubben Edge Cottage, a delightful thatched cottage on your right. This is one of the few thatched cottages still left in Derbyshire.

One of the few thatched cottages still left in Derbyshire

✽ Take the narrow road, Dalebank Lane directly opposite on your left and proceed down hill until reaching the River Amber which flows through the bottom of the valley. Around here, less than half a mile down this lane was the Ashover Light Railway Dalebank station, and if the line is re-instated, Dalebank will be the first of the halts from its starting point in Woolley.

Dalebank Lane where the Ashover Light Railway crossed the road

✱ Now the road begins to rise, so continue uphill until reaching cross roads with Brown Lane to the right and a track with a footpath sign to your left. Take this left hand track which then leads through a stile into a field. Follow this well-defined path which is running close to the original route of the Ashover Light Railway back to Ogston. The path comes out on Dark Lane (**24**) just above Smithy Cottage (**23**) and Sheffield Street (**22**).

✱ Turn left down the hill with the reservoir over to your right. Skirting the water's edge this road had to be lifted to come above water level. Pre-reservoir days, this was where the Ashover Light Railway crossed the road, Woolley station was here and Fox's transport (**27**) left from here. The village petrol pump was positioned here beside Napoleons Home (**28**), the ancient ale house. Now all that is left is Napoleons Cottage on your left. Further along on your right was where the Woolley House/Hydro (**29**) stood. Continue straight ahead as the road begins to rise, passing Oldfield House (**30**) on your left until returning to the car park which is the start/ end of our walk.

4: EASTWOOD – WOODHEAD –
WOOLLEY MOOR – OGSTON - DALEBANK
Walk: 3⅔ miles – 5·8km

A most interesting walk offering some of the most outstanding, far reaching views over the reservoir and surrounding area. The walk incorporates an ancient coaching inn where the local Justice of the Peace held court, the ruins of an ancient hall, the site where Roman coins were found, a toll-bar cottage, and a stately home.

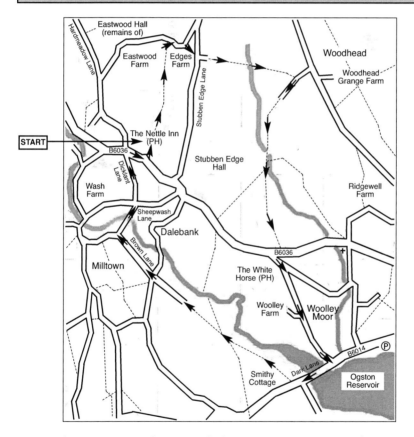

Park in the car park of The Nettle (**35**), an 18th century inn on the B6036 at the junction of Hard Meadow Lane, Ashover, just half a mile from Woolley Moor. Referring to maps, rather confusingly you will find this public house has also been known as The Greyhound, and The Well Run Nettle.

The Nettle Inn

✱ Leave the car-park and turn left, taking the B6036 road towards Woolley for a very short distance until you see a lane on your left with a footpath sign.

✱ Go past the two houses, through Edges Wood and the yard of Edges Farm. At the end of the farm drive you will come to Eastwood Lane. This is where Walk Ten will join. Directly ahead of you is East Wood where a hoard of Roman coins were found in 1922. These included a silver ring and forty three Roman coins of small value. Their

The view over Woodhead Farm from Stubben Edge Lane

period ranged from Septimius Severus (193-211) to Gordianus lll (238-244).

✱ Look to your left and you will see the ruins of Eastwood Hall (**36**) a short distance away down the lane. If you are tempted to take a closer look, take care as the ruins are in a perilous state and should not be entered.

✱ Continue up Eastwood Lane, and at the bend take the footpath that goes off to the right. Pass through the squeeze stile and follow the path through a private wood.

✱ As you reach the brow of the hill pause to admire the scenery. Behind you is the area around Hard Meadow Lane, Ashover and ahead is the view over Ogston which you can admire almost continuously for the next stage of the walk.

The view towards Ogston Reservoir from Stubben Edge Lane

✱ Pass through a squeeze stile onto the road, Stubben Edge Lane also known as Ashover Road. This was the old turnpike road from Tupton, via Stubben Edge Lane to Knot Cross, now Knot Cross Farm, Butterley, and had the distinction of being the shortest turnpike road in the county of Derbyshire. The original board advertising tolls was discovered in the cellar of the Royal Oak, Tupton which stands near the site of the original toll bar cottage, demolished as recently as 1958 to be replaced by a pair of semi-detached houses. It is interesting to note that according to the board, the charges were based on the breadth of a vehicles wheels. The original trustees of this stretch were Joseph Banks of Overton Hall, George Allen esq. of Stubben Edge Hall and Sir Thomas Hunloke of Wingerworth Hall, all owning the land over which the road ran.

✱ Cross the road to another squeeze stile beside the gate and into a field. Cross this field passing the clump of central trees on your right to a wooden stile in the far hedge.

✱ Pass through the woodlands, cross the narrow brook.

✱ Cross the next field towards its middle.

✱ Ascend the next field to the far right hand corner to a stile near the gate of Woodhead Farm. The path from *Walk Three* joins here and the next stage is also in Walk Three.

✱ Pass a small pond and follow the track from the farm around the next field boundary to the top right hand corner where there is a stile.

✱ Aim for the bottom right hand corner of the next field where there is a stile and the perimeter of the garden centre. Keep to the field boundary on your right. In the trees over to your right you will catch a glimpse of Stubben Edge Hall (**37**).

35

Stubben Edge Hall can be seen in the trees

✱ Cross a ditch and bear left at a stile keeping to the field boundary to a stile near the left hand corner of Riley's Chrysanthemums on the B6036. This is Ashover New Road.

✱ Cross the road, skirt the toll-bar cottage (33) and turn into Badger Lane (34). On your right behind the houses is the Jubilee Recreation Ground where the annual Woolley Show (32) is held.

✱ Follow the curve of the road round past Perkins Cottage which was originally a post office/shop. Pass the White Horse Inn (31) and continue down the road towards the reservoir.

✱ As you approach the T junction with Dark Lane, Napoleon's Cottage is on your left. Napoleon's Home (28), the ancient ale house was immediately opposite. As Sam Fox, a lifetime resident of Woolley whose family owned the Napoleon's Home said, *'you could free wheel on your bike down the hill and go straight in through the front door'*.

Down White Horse Lane

The Ashover Light Railway siding bordered the stone wall of the orchard of Napoleon's Home (28) then crossed the B6014 at a gated crossing, one of only two on the line. By the side of the railway line was Amber House (26). The road bridge which crossed the River Amber is traditionally, where Woolley and Woolley Moor meet; the area to the west of the River Amber is

36

Woolley, the area on the east is Woolley Moor.

Floods were recorded on May 25th 1825 when the dam that provided water power for Bump Mill at Kelstedge overflowed and subsequently washed away all the bridges along the River Amber as far down river as Woolley. Apparently the cottages in the Butts were all flooded out, the worst hit being the home of Tommy Nadin the Impounder who had to rescue his wife through the roof.

There is now no trace of Bump Mill (bump is the name given to candlewick) and the dam is currently a private lake in the grounds of Amber House, Kelstedge.

After this 1825 incident Woolley Bridge had to be rebuilt, then one hundred and thirty years later, this stretch of road needed to be raised considerably to bring it above top water-level when the reservoir was built.

If you would like to combine this walk with **Walk One**, turn left and proceed along Dark Lane until on your right you reach the car park, which is the start/end of **Walk One**.

✱ To continue **Walk Four**, turn right and proceed up Dark Lane (**24**) skirting the reservoir until reaching Quarry Lane junction on your left.

Looking up Dark Lane with the junction of Quarry Lane to your left

If you are on **Walk Ten**, continue on Quarry Lane to return to the car park.
✱ To continue Walk Four, cross the road and just after Smithy Cottage, turn right at a footpath sign. Proceed along this footpath and through the valley of Dalebank, passing through six stiles and two gateways. You are walking almost parallel to the track of the Ashover Light Railway (**8**) which ran through this valley.

37

The footpath that leads from the crossroads on Hay Lane across the fields to Dark Lane

✳ Cross Hay Lane and continue straight ahead into Brown Lane until the road branches.

✳ Turn right and follow the road. This is Sheepwash Lane and as the name implies, sheep were brought here to be washed in the River Amber. Clean wool is lighter in weight but fetches more money, so the effort was worthwhile.

✳ After only a few hundred metres, you will pass over another stretch of the ALR disused railway embankment.

✳ Continue straight on at the next cross roads, Hunt Lane. This is an area called Dicklant. Proceed up Dicklant Lane to join the main road opposite The Nettle and the start/end of the walk.

Walking the dogs on Brown Lane

5: OGSTON – HANDLEY – SMITHY MOOR
Walk: 4 miles – 6·3km

A walk through Handley where Miss Peggy Jackson who gave her name to a ALR engine, a lane and the actual railway itself lived. We trace the track of the ALR between Handley Lane through to Ford, along Peggy Lane admiring on the way, the converted Stretton Railway Station now Holly Brook House Smithymoor, and walk back along the east bank of the reservoir.

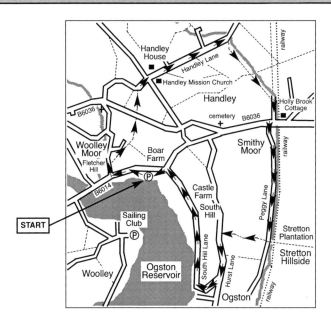

This walk begins at the Car Park on South Hill, to the north of the reservoir on the B6014. Leave the car park and proceed down the road, turning right into Fletcher Hill after Oldfield House. After the garden of Oldfield Barn, go through the stone stile into the field which should be crossed as in Walk Three, passing Handley Field Farm to reach the main B6036. Cross the road, go over the stile and proceed through the fields to Handley Lane. Turn round and admire the view.

Go up the road, passing St Mark's Handley Mission Church on the right. Ignore the roads off to your left and right and walk down the hill towards Clay Cross. Over on your left is Handley House dated 1679. This was the home of Miss Peggy Jackson, one of the daughters of the founder of the Ashover Light Railway.

Handley House, the former home of Miss Peggy Jackson

Proceed down the winding hill until reaching a well-trodden track on your right by the side of Horsecar Brook. Walk in a south-easterly direction. Cross over the brook and walk through a leafy enclosure with the brook flowing on your left. Keep straight ahead following the track passing farmland on either side until the path comes out on the B6104 at Smithymoor Bridge.

Walk along beside Horsecar Brook

Take a look at Holly Brook Cottage the former Stretton Railway Station waiting room and booking office. Passengers for Woolley who alighted here were picked up by Mr Fox, but at the beginning and end of term, the boys of Derby School had to walk from here to the Amber Valley Camp.

Being only a small provincial halt, like many of the local stations it was closed in 1966, but in 1969 was sympathetically converted into a desirable dwelling. It still retains its station appearance and the large, arched cast iron waiting room window which adorns the front elevation.

40

The former Stretton Station, now Holly Brook Cottage

✱ Cross the road and almost directly opposite is the entrance to the Severn Trent Water Plant. It's now a private road with barriers at the far end for the use of the water board personnel only. This was originally the track bed of the ALR (**8**) and is named Peggy Lane after Peggy, the ALR engine. The whole line was often called the Peggy Line which in turn was named after Colonel Jackson's eldest daughter Margaret, Beatrice Meinertzhagen Jackson known to everyone as Peggy. Miss Peggy Jackson lived at Handley House that we passed earlier. She was a highly respected lady, Guide Commissioner and a close personal friend of Lady Olave Baden-Powell, the Chief Guide who stayed at Handley House when in the area.

Her name-sake Peggy the steam engine was probably the best known of the locomotives and had the dubious honour of taking the last steam train on the ALR on July 5th 1949. She was taken out of stock in 1950 and one of the nameplates is now preserved at the Narrow Gauge Railway Museum at Tywyn.

Peggy Lane

Lady Baden-Powell

Follow Peggy Lane which runs parallel to the brook until reaching a footpath on your right and one on your left. If you are on Walk Eight A from Stretton and have walked down the hillside from the A61, this is where you will join **Walk Five**.

Take the right footpath, away from Stretton hillside and walk through the next three fields over the stiles provided until emerging on Crow Lane. Turn left. Pass the reservoir houses. This area was Ford and this is the old Ford Lane, a bridleway connecting Ford with Ogston, and where the River Amber originally forded giving the hamlet its name.

The route ahead now passes through part of the Severn Trent Water Authority's Treatment Plant, but take the right fork into Hurst Lane. Pass the garden wall of Ford House (7) on your left. When you encounter a white iron fence on your left, pause to take a closer look at the dam wall (5) and Ogston Reservoir (1) stretched out ahead of you.

Continue along Hurst Lane which becomes South Hill Lane bordering the reservoir all the way until emerging at South Hill on the B6014. Turn left and walk down the hill a short distance until arriving at the car park which is the start/end of our walk.

The dam wall

For those on **Walk Eight A**, follow the route of **Walk Five** from here, through Handley and Smithy Moor, and leave the route on Peggy Lane where you joined it

The view over the reservoir from South Hill Lane

42

6: OGSTON CARR

Walk: 2½ miles – 3·9km

A promenade along the western edge of the reservoir, a bird-hide, a pleasant rural walk with magnificent views over the reservoir and Brackenfield Church.

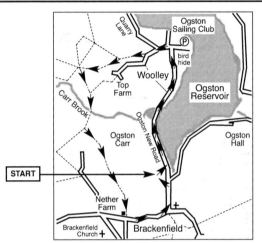

This walk starts from the car park on the end of Ogston New Road (13) at Brackenfield, and the first part follows the road which runs along the west bank of Ogston reservoir (1). Look across the reservoir to the dam wall (5), at the right hand side of which is Ogston Hall (6) although it's virtually obscured by the trees. This road provides an ideal vantage point for watching the yachts or local bird life although the marginal trees cause a lot of obstruction particularly when in leaf.

Walking along Ogston New Road provides some ideal vantage points for watching the yachts

43

*In winter the bare trees
allow tantalising glimpses
across the water, but in summer
these views are almost obscured*

Just after the road narrows and the footpath peters out, the road makes a sharp bend and veering to the right is the west car park where you will find a bird-hide belonging to the Ogston Bird Club (**15**). It's open to the public, so go inside and sit on one of the six benches placed in front of the fourteen small windows. Be quiet and patient and you may be rewarded with a glimpse of some rare species.

*The unmade road off Quarry Lane, looking
towards the back of the Old Chapel,
Draycott's Holdings and old path*

Inside the Ogston bird hide

After this slight detour, leave the car park and head up the road which has now become Quarry Lane. Pass the Sailing Club (**16**) on your right. At the bend, leave the road and take the unmade road straight ahead. Pass Revell Farm and Yew Tree Farm (**18-19**) and continue until the road forks. Take the right fork and continue until reaching a T junction. Turn left then after a short distance you will see a stone stile on the right. Go through this into the field. Cross the field in the direction of the copse – Fibredole Wood – in the distance. When reaching the field before the copse, head towards the right hand corner of the wood. Go through the stile and round the wood's edge, over the first fence and to the top corner of the wall in the second field. Climb over this into the next field and follow the field's edge to the stile.

Once through this, the path then follows the wall down the next field which drops sharply to Carr Brook in the dip. A stone stile hidden by holly trees opens onto a stone footbridge across Carr Brook. Go over this then head up the field keeping the hedgerow to your left. About half way up the field, the hedgerow peters out. Turn left here, cutting straight across the next field. Look for a stone stile concealed in the wall at the edge of Ogston Carr Wood. This wood has been leased by the Derbyshire Naturalist Trust, and is now a well-wardened natural reserve to which there is no admittance. Go through this stile and down across the stream in the dip, up the bank side and the stone steps to emerge into a field. Cross this field following the fence along the edge of Ogston Carr Wood. Carr Farm is over to your right.

Go over the stile in the corner of the field and proceed across the next field, through a stile at the edge of some holly bushes. Once through this, walk

along the edge of the next field, keeping the hedgerow to your left. Proceed across the fields, skirting the corner of Ogston Carr Wood, and then along a track which brings you out on Church Lane, Brackenfield (**11**), next to Nether Farm. This is the site of one of the five Brackenfield Well Dressings.

Turn left down Church Lane until reaching Brackenfield Church. Turn left along Ogston New Road, passing Church Farm on your left, then Ogston Lodge (**12**) opposite the gates to Ogston Hall to return to the car park on your left.

Brackenfield Church

45

7: OGSTON – BRACKENFIELD –
MATHERS GRAVE – TRINITY CHAPEL - OXON
Walk: 4½ miles – 6·75km

From the car park by the Ogston Sailing Club, walk beside the reservoir to Brackenfield. Discover the largest village green in the country and use the millennium pump to draw fresh water the way the villagers used to do. Learn the mystery behind the hamlet named Mathers Grave, explore an ancient chapel ruin and walk back through the fields on a 13th century track called Chirchegate, used by the people of Oxon who attended the old Trinity Chapel.

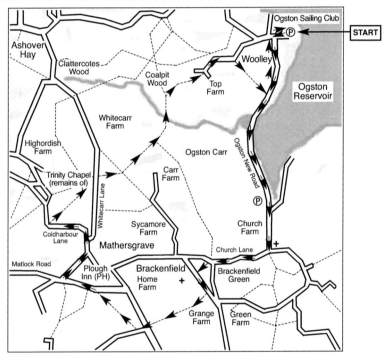

This walk starts from the car park just past Ogston Sailing Club (16 -17) situated at the junction of Quarry Lane and Ogston New Road (13). Before leaving the car park look across the reservoir. The views from here are over the north and east banks of the reservoir. Over to your left is Oldfield House and further round, its just possible to see the cottages opposite the north car park and visually follow South Hill along the eastern shore round to the reservoir dam with Ogston Hall almost hidden in the trees. In the corner of the car park is a stone built bird hide which is open to the public.

*The view from the west car park across the reservoir.
Over to the right of the boat is Oldfield House*

✻ Leave the car park and turn left to walk along the western edge of the reservoir until reaching Brackenfield. At the T junction with Holy Trinity Church (**11B**) on your left, turn right into Church Lane, Brackenfield. Proceed up the hill until you reach Brackenfield Green, the largest village green in the county. The Green is triangular in shape. On the northern side is the Village School which is now the Parish Hall, and on the western side is the Methodist Church. Situated on The Green in front of the old village school is a stone trough and pump which on closer inspection has a plaque commemorating the fact that it was re-instated on the site of the original village water supply in 1999 as part of the villages millennium celebrations. It's a real gem from the past and its working too, so draw yourself a cool, fresh drink. This pump holds special significance to the well-dressing celebrations that take place here every year. (**11**).

*The Millenium pump drawing water from the original
village well has been re-instated*

47

Walk to almost the end of the green, veering to your right to take the bridle path sign to Matlock Road. On reaching Matlock Road, the busiest stretch of road you'll encounter on this walk,. Cross over to take the narrow Lindway Lane and after a short distance, a footpath to the right which will bring you out further up Matlock Road, opposite the Plough Inn.

The Plough Inn
is an old farmhouse full of character

Cross the road and continue for a short distance up the main road then turn right into Mathersgrave Lane leading to the hamlet of Mathersgrave. Its rather unusual to find such a pretty hamlet with such an unappealing though intriguing name, and apparently it's all to do with a chap called Samuel Mather.

You will now approach a T junction. To your right is School Lane which leads back to Brackenfield, to your left is Whitecarr Lane which leads to Dark Lane, but note the high wall on your left. By the set-in gate post are two square stones. They are hard to decipher but the top stone has the initials SM and the lower stone the date 1643. This is the reason for the hamlets name – Mathersgrave.

One source states that Samuel Mather was hanged for sheep stealing; another that he committed suicide in an old barn not far from Brackenfield Green. The latter is backed by various entries in Morton register that state that he took his own life after the birth of an illegitimate daughter who financially he could not support. In those days such cases were provided for by the parish, and the stigma attached could have been just too much for Samuel.

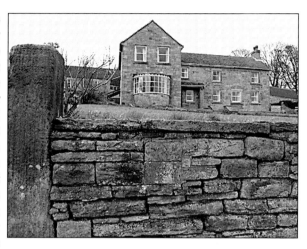

Mathers grave stones

Suicides, criminals, suspect witches and other undesirables could not be buried in consecrated ground and were regularly buried at cross-roads to show their marginal status in society. However, it's unclear where Samuel's last resting place was to be because there's an additional bit to the story.

According to local legend, Samuel's body was being drawn to his grave by bullocks but they suddenly stopped and a raven ominously settled on his corpse. This was an age when incredulity and ignorance was rife. All black birds were associated with darkness and evil, and viewed with suspicion, but the raven was the most feared because it was believed to be the shape adopted by the devil. Understandably the men accompanying the corpse were totally freaked. They considered it to be an omen of such gargantuan significance that they refused to go one step further and Samuel was hurriedly buried on the spot. He would have remained there indefinitely if his body hadn't been found while the road was being widened. That's why Samuel Mather was re-interred under the wall of the cottage garden, the two rather crudely carved stones mark the spot and the hamlet adopted the name Mathers Grave.

But back to the walk! Turn left into Whitecarr Lane, then left at the fork ahead into Cold Harbour Lane. Continue up this road, round the bend of Trinity Farm and a little further look for a stile in the wall on the right. Pass through the coppice and out into a field taking the path down the hillside where on your left, hidden amongst the trees are the ruins of Trinity Chapel. **(11A)**

Trinity Chapel ruins

View from Trinity Chapel

In the country, be aware of other road users

Walk down the field out onto the road – Carr Lane. From here there are some superb views over the whole of Ogston Reservoir and the surrounding countryside.

Turn right then down the track immediately to the left. It is believed that this track is a very old lane that in the 13th century was named Chirchegate meaning a lane leading to a church or chapel and ran across the valley from Oxon (**19**) to Trinity Chapel.

The old track believed to be Chirchegate, dating from the 13th century

There are tremendous views from Chirchegate

To take this ancient route walk down the track which continues down two fields to meet a farm track which leads to Carr Farm. Just at this bend, walk along the field to the left (Carr Farm is to the right), through the stile at the side of the gate, turning into the field to the right. Follow the hedgerow until eventually it comes out into the right hand corner of this field. Here another path comes in from the left.

Turn right and walk down the fields following the hedgerows to come to a stone footbridge over Carr Brook. Go over this, up the field, across the track and up to the stile. Head down the road, around the bend on the right, to the small driveway entrance to Walnut Cottage. Go down here and look for the stile and gateway to the left of the first farm building. Go through this and across the fields to come out onto Ogston New Road. Turn left to return to the car park which is on your right and the start/end of this walk.

8 A: STRETTON – STRETTON HILLSIDE – OGSTON HANDLEY – SMITHY MOOR
Walk: 5 miles – 7·9km

8 B: HIGHAM – HIGHAM HILLSIDE – BRACKENFIELD – OGSTON
Walk: 4¾ miles – 7·5km

WALK EIGHT A

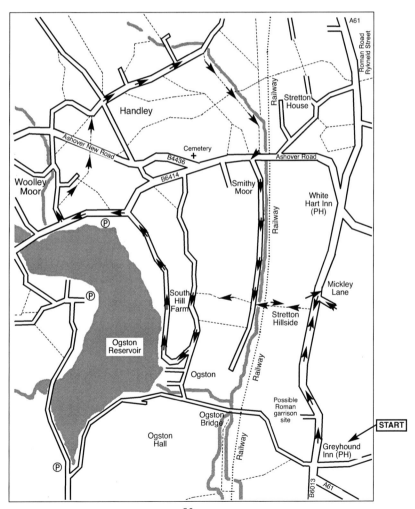

Since the construction of the railway line that crosses the valley from north to south, there are only a few places in this area where it is possible to leave the A61, follow the old pack horse routes down the hillside and cross the railway line. The most northerly is the B6014 – Ashover Road at Stretton. To take this, turn by the White Hart Inn. This is the route of the old Turnpike Road and will take you straight through to Ogston.

The most southerly route is down Bumpmill Lane at the far end of Higham which gets its name from the Bump (candlewick) Mill that was situated close to the present railway bridge. Like many of these local mills, it obtained its power from the water of the River Amber. Bumpmill Lane leads to the A615 Matlock road at Wessington. On Walk Seven we actually cross this road a little further along.

Between these two roads are two footpaths and a bridleway almost equally spaced. To use these footpaths, we suggest starting at the Greyhound Inn, just before the A61 meets the B6013 at Higham.

For convenience, we have joined each of these walks to existing walks. *Walk Eight A* from Stretton joins *Walk Five*. *Walk Eight B* from Higham joins *Walk One*.

WALK EIGHT A

To follow the footpath from Stretton, begin your walk at The Greyhound Inn at Higham (**9**) and walk along the Main Road towards Stretton. This is the route of the old Roman road Rykneld Street, one of the most important Roman roads through Britain. It began near Bourton on the Water in Gloucestershire as a northern route for the Fosse Way, terminating at Templeborough Roman Fort near Rotherham in Yorkshire. Stretton or Straettum as it was recorded in 1002 is derived from the Old English meaning 'Farm on the Roman Road'.

Roman coins have been found around here, and its almost certain that the Romans had a garrison stationed here. The most likely location for this is across the other side of the road on what is now the Water Board Site.

Continue walking along the main road until reaching a right turn to Mickley. The walk can begin here, but as it is not permitted to park on the main road it is necessary to park on Mickley Lane.

Cross to the left of the bus stop (to Clay Cross) on the A61. Here you will find a track marked with a footpath sign. The track falls away immediately at a sharp angle to the road. Looking down you'll see five posts preventing vehicular access, with a squeeze stile to the left. This track goes through a small hedged area, crosses another stile and opens onto Stretton hillside. Enjoy the views. Head for the first electricity pylon from the right and at the bottom of the field is a white wooden stile. Cross Smithy Brook and the railway line by the allocated route and enter Stretton plantation where it is necessary to cross another brook. The footpath leaves the plantation and joins

Roman soldiers would have been familiar with this area

Peggy Lane, the track bed of the ALR. Here you can join Walk Five which will take you through Ford and along South Hill Lane to emerge at the B6014. Turn left to follow the circular route of **Walk Five** through Handley and Smithy Moor and leave the route on Peggy Lane where you joined it.

WALK EIGHT B

This walk begins at the car park of the Greyhound Inn, just before the A61 meets the B6013 at Higham (**9**). Leave the car park, cross the road and veer left. Directly opposite Well Lane you will find a gated, surfaced drive. This is Ogston Lane.

WALK EIGHT B

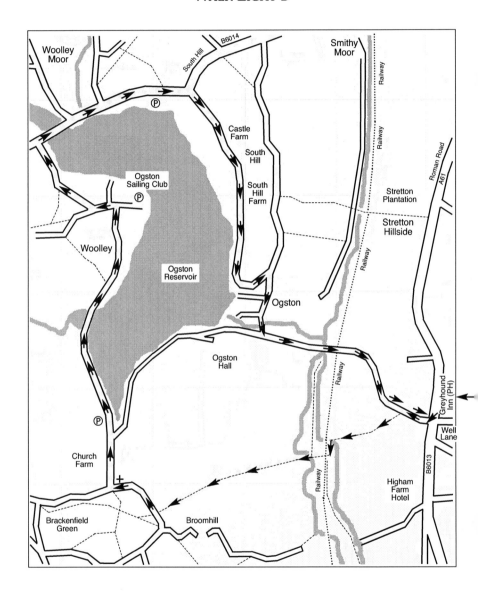

The Higham entrance to Ogston Hall

On your left at the end of Ogston Lane, numbers 13, 14 & 15 comprise the old Higham Hall. Number 14 possesses some attractive hood mouldings that project over the lower windows. This may be some of the oldest stonework in the village dating from c.1500.

The entrance to Ogston Lane

Possibly one of the oldest properties in Higham

Ogston Lane has always been a private carriage-way for Ogston Hall (**6**). It goes down Higham Hillside (**10**), crosses the railway and river and arrives at the back gates of the Hall.

Proceed down this lane and after approximately ¼ mile, take the footpath over a stile on the left leaving the lane to take a well defined path through the field. Continue downhill towards the main railway line in the valley bottom.

The delightful walk down Ogston Lane

Turn left and after a short distance, cross the railway by the footbridge provided. This is the joining point of **Walk One**. Your route will now pass through Brackenfield, go all round the reservoir and back to Ogston Lane.

9: CLATTERCOTES – HIGHORDISH – COFFIN ROAD – OVERTON HALL – GIN LANE – MILLTOWN – OGSTON

Walk: 6 miles – 9·4km

The effort needed for this rather strenuous uphill climb to Highordish, is rewarded by the tremendous views over the valley, that you can enjoy for most of the walk.

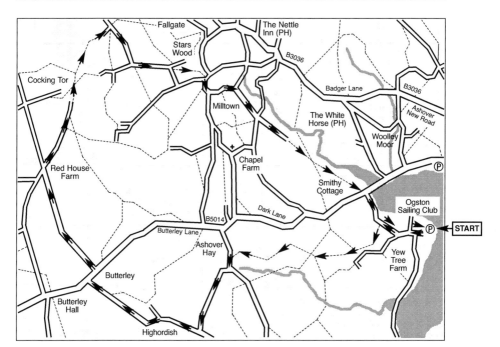

Our walk begins at the west car-park of Ogston Reservoir on Quarry Lane. Leave the car-park and walk up Quarry Lane, then just before the Old Methodist Chapel, take the footpath to your left into the fields. Ascend the field past the edge of a field on your right and aim for the far right-hand corner of the field where there is a stile. The views back to the reservoir and beyond are particularly attractive from here. Turn right along the walled path for a few hundred yards to a stile. Turn left along the left hand side of the field for a few yards before turning right and cross the field on a defined path. Ascend three stiles to reach the right hand side of a wood. The path is well defined as you continue ahead to a stile and path sign. Bear left to more stiles

59

Clattercotes Farm is on the site of Clattercotes Hall

before walking through Clattercotes Farm.

Clattercotes Farm was built on the site of Clattercotes Hall. One former resident, Hugh Willoughby, could have been as famous as Drake and Raleigh. He was Britain's first Arctic explorer in command of three vessels sent out in 1554 to discover a route to China and the East. He and his crew became stranded off the coast of Lapland and froze to death. Their bodies were discovered a year later.

Reaching the road, turn left and descend. In 140 yards turn right into Berridge Lane. In a short distance, approach a ford. On your left is Clattercotes Wood. Ascend the lane past Berrisford Lane Farm dated 1693. Follow the lane round to your left and just before Highordish Farm on your left, take the footpath to the right marked – Car Park. This will bring you to the car park and picnic site at Highordish on Coldharbour Lane. This site is situated on a heather and bilberry clad hillside overlooking Ogston reservoir and some of the finest views in Derbyshire. On very clear days Bolsover Castle and Hardwick Hall are regularly recorded, and some people claim to have seen as far as the Humber bridge.

Leave the car park and turn right along Coldharbour Lane. It's a rather bleak place. Cross the main road Butterly Lane B6014. Turn right then left along Holestonegate Road. At a staggered crossing by Red House Farm, branch to the right heading N.NE. This is Coffin Road, the route taken by coffin bearers from the neighbouring hamlets of Lea and Dethick. Although in the parish of Ashover until the late 19th century, these outlying districts were without their own burial grounds, so the corpses were taken to Ashover for

The view from Highordish

burial. In **Walk Two** we mentioned this route which can be viewed from the Jubilee Recreation Ground at Woolley.

Over to your left is a chapel-like building known as Moscow or Moscar. The name Moscow or Moscar identifies a topographical feature and the site's vegetation. 'Mos' is a swamp or bog which has a very distinctive appearance and 'kian' is wet ground overgrown with rushes. Ahead is Cocking Tor, a very prominent rock feature known locally as Gladstone's

Nose because of the uncanny resemblance to that esteemed statesman. From here a most impressive view down over Ashover and the Amber Valley can be obtained.

Follow the well trodden path past the old chimney on your right. This is an area called White Hillocks and bears the scars of earlier lead mining activity. The White Hillocks are spoil heaps

A cyclist on the Coffin Way

from Gregory Mine, it's name derived from the debris of old lead workings which were composed of sparkling white crystals of Calcite and Calc-spar. On a sunny day, their almost luminous whiteness was visible for miles around, but several periods of re-working for the mineral content has removed much

Be prepared to make some new friends on your walks!

of the sparkling material and the hillocks have lost their lustre.

To your left is Robin Hood's Mark although there is no evidence to link this rock outcrop which is over 900 ft above sea level with the famous outlaw. The rock measures 26 ft in circumference and has an estimated weight of 14 tons.

According to local legend, when Ashover clock strikes midnight, this great rock turns, thus the name, the

Turning Stone. At any other time it is impossible to turn the stone manually although it will rock to and fro upon its precarious pedestal by applying surprisingly little pressure.

The path now continues through the Forestry Commission plantation and emerges onto Gin Lane. Turn right and over on your left is Overton Hall where the evacuated boys from Derby School were originally billeted. This thirty roomed hall has a chequered past as a home, a school, a youth hostel, a residential home for the elderly, an approved school and of course, as a temporary school for the boys of Derby School before they were moved to Amber Valley Camp. It's most famous owner was Joseph Banks who in 1768-71 accompanied Captain James Cook aboard HMS Endeavour acting as the supervisory scientist on the Royal Society's famed expedition to the South Seas. It is now divided into private apartments.

Continue down Gin Lane until reaching Milltown and The Miner's Arms. Turn right up Oakstedge Lane, then left onto Brown Lane. At the crossroads with Hay Lane and Dalebank Lane, continue straight ahead down the track which will bring you out just above Smithy Cottage on Dark Lane. Cross the road and turn down Quarry Lane. Follow this road until reaching the car-park and the start/end of the walk.

Overton Hall

63

10: OGSTON TO ASHOVER FOLLOWING THE TRACK OF THE ALR

Walk: 6 miles – 9·4km

Because many people are interested in the Ashover Light Railway and the route it took from Clay Cross to Ashover, we thought it would be an idea to retrace that route as far as possible on the first stages of this walk. On **Walk Five** and **Walk Eight A** we followed the trackbed from Smithy Moor on Peggy Lane and touched it again round Ford. On **Walk One** and **Walk Eight B** we picked up the track bed around Ford to the point where it disappeared under the reservoir. On **Walk Ten** we will pick it up again at the other side of the reservoir and follow it through to Ashover. The trackbed in many places along its route can still be clearly defined but as the land on which it lies is owned by private individuals, we would be trespassing.

Instead, here is our alternative, circular route passing through some of the most delightful scenery and calling at Ashover, one of the most popular and pretty villages in the area, before returning to Ogston.

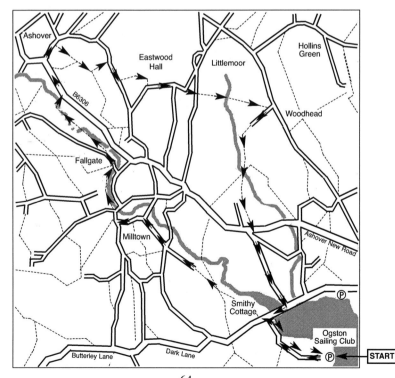

64

Our walk begins at the west car park of Ogston Reservoir, proceeds along Quarry Lane and joins the B6014 at Dark Lane. Turn left and cross the road where just after Smithy Cottage (**23**) is a footpath sign by a stone stile.

If the ALRS scheme goes ahead and a line is run from Ogston, the first stage would be from Ogston to Dalebank. Originally this was one of the most scenic stretches of the route and ran from Woolley Bridge, climbing through the wide valley where trees came down almost to the sides of the line. The River Amber, originally on the left was crossed twice within ¼ mile then ran beside the track as far as Dale Bank Lane, where, after crossing the lane came to a halt at Dalebank station. This is where mushrooms grew in such profusion that the early morning train crews would slow the locomotive to walking pace (the maximum speed was 25 m.p.h.) in order to climb down and gather them.

In order to follow this stretch of the ALR route as closely as possible, take the footpath above Smithy Cottage. In Walks Three and Four we walked this path from the Dalebank end. Take the well worn path through a copse and out through a stile. Walk along the top edge of the field following the path by the wall on the left hand side. Woolley Moor can be seen over to the right, and in the field in the foreground is a capped, disused mine-shaft. The path continues through a gap between holly trees, across another field, through a stile and over one more field in the corner of which adjacent to the gate is a stile. You are now on a track which leads out onto Dalebank Lane.

To follow the next stage of the route and arrive at Milltown which was the next stop ¼ mile away, walk straight ahead along Brown Lane until it comes

The Milltown pinfold

65

out on Oakstedge Lane, Milltown. Just to your right across this road is the village pinfold, a stone enclosure used for holding stray animals that belonged to the villagers. In order to retrieve them, their owners had to pay a fine to the village impounder.

Between the pinfold and the Miners Arms is Gin Lane. This is not a publicity stunt by the Miners Arms to promote the colourless liquid that goes with tonic. This gin is short for engine, and was the name given to a primitive engine driven by horses, the type that would have been employed in the areas numerous mines. The area is rich in mineral deposits particularly fluorspar and lead, and Milltown has a very strong lead mining tradition. The land around Gin Lane has been greatly disturbed over the years and we are left with evidence of this in the many abandoned mines most of which are now capped and hidden in the undergrowth.

It's therefore unsurprising that Milltown's inn should be named the Miners Arms to perpetuate the history of the area, although this 17th century building was once called The Regulator, probably a reference to the mechanism that controlled the fluid flow of the pumping engines at the lead mines.

During the boom in Derbyshire lead mining in the eighteenth and nineteenth centuries, something of the rowdy spirit of the wild west reigned. This may have been largely due to the huge amount of ale consumed, as ale was believed to be an antidote to lead poisoning. Even in those days, the toxicity of lead was known to be a problem for both people and livestock, so understandably the miners rejoiced in consuming great quantities of medicinal ale. In order to cater for this need, the doors of the Miners Arms were open for business every day from 6am to 10pm.

The old track bed of the ALR which ran by the side of the Miners Arms, Milltown, and from where the train emerged blind due to the close proximity of the buildings, now seen through a barrier of trees

66

Originally the railway at Milltown was to have run much closer to the river, but to avoid the risk of flooding, the track was actually laid much further west of the proposed course which meant that it ran alongside the boundary wall of the Miners Arms. There was no gated crossing on Oakstedge Lane and as the building and the high wall obscured the train crews vision, it meant that any train approaching from Fallgate, did so blind. This was extremely hazardous, causing many narrow escapes and at least one collision.

Leaving Milltown the track turned north to run through a tree shaded cutting almost parallel to the river and after approximately a quarter of a mile entered the Overton estate and the dusty confines of Fallgate Quarry and Milltown fluorspar washing plant.

Walk beside the river parallel to the road and the former track of the ALR

*A well-concealed gem – the old Fallgate Station
and a stretch of the ALR track lies beside the path*

67

We can use the footpath that runs from Milltown alongside the river and road to Fallgate where there is a well concealed gem – the old ALR Fallgate station and a short stretch of track.

Almost overgrown with ivy on the outside, the rampant vegetation is even

The ALR Station at Fallgate is almost overrun with vegetation

inside the buildings, but this doesn't detract from the pleasure of seeing what these old stations were actually like in situ. There is a story that a local farmer, expecting a poultry shed to be delivered on the ALR, mistakenly tried to take the Dalebank station building. Looking at this survivor from the past at Fallgate, it's not difficult to see why.

After the closure of the ALR, the Fallgate shunting yard remained in operation which might account for why these original buildings and section of track have survived. It is now reclamation land.

Leaving Fallgate, the railway line turned north west to be hemmed in by a moss covered wall on one side and the river on the other. We will leave the former Fallgate quarry on Jetting Street, a bridle way that feeds up the hillside, but ignoring this, turn right, cross the bridge and walk back onto the main road opposite Smithy Farm. Turn left until you reach the T junction with Hockley Lane. Turn left and walk along this road until encountering a broad path on your left which leads to Fallgate Mill, now often referred to as Fall Mill. The present building dates from 1731 but is a rebuild of an earlier mill. The mill was operated as recently as 1961 and is the only one of Ashovers four mills to be preserved although as a safety precaution, the mill pond was filled in and the old mill wheel is gradually being overpowered by vegetation Originally intended for grinding grain into flour, around 1925 the mill began grinding fluorspar for the Clay Cross Company. Because fluorspar was so hard, the dust was used as a flux in the making of glass and as an additive to paint used for roadmarkings. Much harder millstones were needed to grind the fluorspar and there are a couple lying around near the mill which is open to the public upon request to Ashover Parish Council.

Fallgate Mill

69

An abandoned mill stone

The plaque   *The mill wheel*

Walk past the mill and following the path towards the River Amber, cross a foot bridge and climb the flight of steps. Turn right at the top and turn almost immediately to go through Demonsdale Farm.

Leave the mill and cross the river

A public footpath leading to Abraham's Lane provides a very pleasant walk along this stretch of the River Amber which remains so pure, it is able to support crayfish and brown trout. Abraham's Lane crosses the river by a bridge made of slabs, then bears right to where the remains of a bridge constructed for the ALR can be seen.

The gradient of the ALR route had steepened to 1 in 58 past the old mill and as the Amber became more sinuous, bridges carried the track from one side to the other. We will leave the valley and the ALR route by a path which ascends to join Hockley Lane almost opposite Hockley Cottage. This was built between 1671-76 by Leonard Wheatcroft one of Ashover's most famous sons. Under the eaves in front of the house is a stone bearing the date and the initials LW and EW, his wife Elizabeth.

The footpath on Hockley Lane comes out almost opposite Hockley Cottage

Turn left and just as you reach the village, look out for a footpath sign on your left which takes us down to the ALR next stop Salter Lane. Geographically this is the closest point to Ashover, but access is via a steep tarmac path called Hollow Lane.

Leaving Salter Lane the railway continued at 1 in 80 for another half mile and skirted The Butts before running into the terminus at Ashover Butts. The name Butts probably dates from the 14th century when all able bodied men were expected to be proficient with the Longbow, ready to be called upon in case of a national disaster. By Royal decree, Sunday afternoons were set aside for archery practice in a designated area known as The Butts after the target used for shooting at

To view this section of the disused track, walk round The Poet's Corner and continue into Butts Road. At the end of the row of houses on your left, a track goes down the hill past the sewage treatment works, over the River Amber and another section of the track.

Retrace your steps along Butts Road and turn up Church Street. Pass the village tuck shop on your left, then the church next to which is the Crispin Inn. Further up the road is the Black Swan.

Turn up Church Street passing the Old Tuck Shop on your left

The same view c1907

Ashover from the graveyard with the Crispin in the foreground and the Black Swan behind. Round the corner to your left is the Post Office and a family butcher

Directly opposite the Crispin Inn is the Basset rooms beside which is a well defined and stiled path. Continue, skirting the playing fields until reaching the Rectory Fields where the annual Ashover Show is held in August.

The Bassett Rooms

Looking back down the path to the church and the Bassett Rooms

Leave the showground by the well-defined public footpath across the field, branching left at the T junction. Take the path across two fields until reaching a stone stile in the wall. This brings you out on Hard Meadow Lane.

Two views from Hard Meadows Lane. Above, the footpath through the fields to Ashover. Below, the view towards Edges Farm with the ivy-covered ruins of Eastwood Hall to your left

Turn right then after about 200 metres turn left on the foot path just before Eastwood House Farm. Follow the path by the side of the hedge through the next fields, then on reaching the farm, turn right in front of the farmhouse which is built into the ruins of Eastwood Hall. Ahead of you is Eastwood Lane. Turn left up the lane passing the ruins on your left and proceed until reaching the entrance to Edges Farm on your right. At this point we suggest you join *Walk Four* – Eastwood – Woodhead – Woolley Moor, leaving the walk at the junction of Dark Lane and Quarry Lane to return to the car park.

The ruins of Eastwood Hall

1 OGSTON RESERVOIR

Due to the considerable expansion during the immediate post-war years, (1945-50) it was obvious that in order to supply the amount of water required in North East Derbyshire, a new major source had to be located. This became urgent when the National Coal Board constructed the Avenue Carbonisation Plant at Wingerworth, as they needed a supply of 1.0mgd to be available by November 1955.

Various potential sources within the area were considered and it was finally decided in August 1953 to carry out a full-scale investigation of an impounding reservoir at Ogston. Trail boring on the site commenced in December 1953 and on March 5th 1954, the North East Derbyshire Joint Water Committee voted to go ahead with the scheme. An application was made to the Ministry for an Order in August 1954, and sanction to proceed was obtained in December 1954. The cost of the scheme was estimated at over £860,000.

Great concern was aroused and many protests were made. The target date of November 1955 set by the National Coal Board meant that any opposition to the Order could not be prolonged, so every effort was made to reach agreement with all concerned prior to the official hearing.

76

Consultations took place with the Trent River Board, the various riparian owners and land owners, the Ministry of Agriculture and Fisheries, the Council for the Preservation of Rural England, and the Derbyshire County Council.

Richard Turbutt of Ogston Hall, a major land owner was a member of the Rural District Council and had originally suggested the possibility of a reservoir on his land.

A letter dated March 3rd 1954 from the North East Derbyshire Joint Water Committee was sent to Richard Turbutt after it had been decided to proceed with the reservoir scheme. It included the following passage:-

"The committee particularly desire me to convey to you their very sincere appreciation of the ready co-operation and assistance you have shown throughout the preliminary examination of the scheme. This co-operation has been invaluable to the Committee and their Officers in the preparation of what is an urgent and complex proposal and it is a matter of pleasure to the Committee that you have felt able to respond to their suggestion in so public spirited a way."

Twenty four properties were acquired by the Committee. Five of these properties were demolished and inundated, and the remainder were sufficiently near to the top water level to make them unsuitable for continued habitation.

The view across the valley towards South Hill

The stone from the buildings was used to make walls round the western boundaries of the reservoir and Hawkins of Woolley removed the slates and internal features which were taken to their reclamation yard at Cromford Hill.

Work on Ogston Reservoir began in February 1955 but the estimated cost had now risen from £860,000 to £1,300,000. This included raising the B6014 Stretton -Matlock road to bring it above top water level, and the construction of a new stretch of road replacing the submerged strip linking Brackenfield and Woolley.

The reservoir was to have a capacity of 1,360 million gallons, a surface area of 210 acres and a maximum depth of 60 feet.

The scheme consisted of an embankment or dam wall on the River Amber

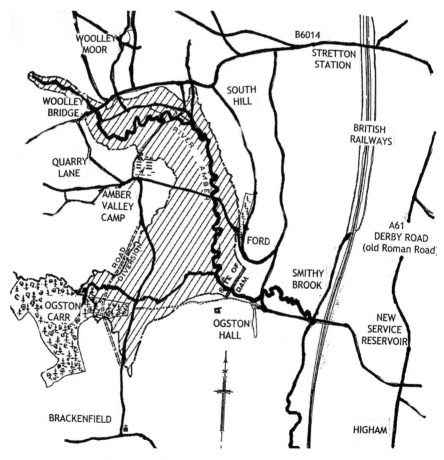

The proposed area to be covered by Ogston reservoir

together with ancillary works, treatment plant, pumping station, service reservoir at Higham and the associated trunk mains required to carry the water into the supply areas. The main contract was given to Messrs Lehanne, Mackenzie & Shand Ltd.

Fourteen miles of mains were laid, including a 45cm (18 inch) diameter rising main from the pumping station to the Higham Service reservoir. Made by the Staveley Iron and Chemical Company Ltd, these are all spun iron pipes except where they cross the main railway adjacent to Ogston Lane from Stretton. Here they are made of 45cm (18 inch) diameter steel pipe. In total nine railway crossings and eight river crossings were involved.

By December 1957, the reservoir had risen to a height of 30 feet yet ironically, the heat wave in Derbyshire had brought water restrictions in June and in a bid to save water, a shut-off period was imposed from seven thirty each evening to five thirty next morning. 1957 was another abnormally dry summer and the Committee were experiencing difficulties obtaining sufficient water from their other supplies. By September 17th, the drought had reached record proportions having run for thirty five days.

During the long, hot spell, the remains of Derwent Hall, demolished in 1943 and submerged under Ladybower Reservoir were exposed, yet water from Ogston was distributed throughout the area as far north as Frecheville and Gleadless on the edge of Sheffield. Even though the treatment plant was considerably overloaded, a constant supply of water was delivered through August, September, October and November.

The reservoir first overflowed on February 26th 1960, and the official inauguration of the reservoir by Alderman Mrs G Burton, took place on Saturday April 9th 1960.

2 THE MATLOCK TO MANSFIELD TURN-PIKE ROAD

In 1555, the repair of the highways was made the responsibility of each parish, with every parishioner performing four days labour on the roads each year as his statute duty. Although this was later increased to six days, this form of maintenance was not effective and many roads were in bad repair until in 1706/7 the first turnpike trusts were authorised. The trusts were made up of local landowners, wealthy merchants who had a vested interest in the roads or those who wished to loan money on the basis of an annuity in exchange for maintaining stretches of road paid for by the users.

The B6014 was part of the Matlock to Mansfield turnpike road also known as the Tansley to Tibshelf Turnpike. It ran from Tansley through Woolley

Bridge to the staggered junction of what is now the A61 at Stretton. The name Stretton means settlement on the Roman Road – Rykneld Street which ran along the high ridge above the River Amber.

The roads were also used by a great many animals being driven to markets, fairs, fattening grounds or between grazing fields. Not only did these herds slow down traffic, they damaged the road surface and soiled the highway with excrement.

In order for the Royal Mail coaches to maintain higher than average speeds, it was imperative that they travelled at night when it was rare to find animals on the road. In 1757 it took three days to travel from Derby to London and by 1777 there was a daily service which cost £1.8s for inside passengers. Mail coaches were legally exempt from toll fees and would announce their approach with a sharp blast on the post horn in order that the toll bars or gates would be opened in readiness. Travel was far from comfortable and often roads were so steep and difficult to ascend that it was impossible for horses to drag their loaded coaches. It was therefore common for the driver to request the passengers to alight and walk or even help to push, a common occurrence when leaving the sunken basin of the Amber Valley.

Dark Lane, the area either side of Woolley Bridge would have been an important staging post on the turnpike road because it had a Smithy and a Wheelwrights, as necessary in those days as our modern day service stations. Coupled with these, there was also the inn, appropriately called The Traveller's Rest where food and rest was provided for man and beast before the long haul up either side of the valley.

Evidence points to the fact that there was a turnpike cottage in this area to collect the tolls from road users, and according to Mr Sam Fox the cottage was later used as a dame school before being demolished.

3 MILL LANE

Mill Lane branched off Hurst Lane and ran north/north-east across the valley to Woolley Mill, also known as Revell's Mill. Later when the Amber Valley Camp was built, Mill Lane ran straight through the centre of the camp.

A pleasing feature of this lane was the little spring that bubbled up at the roadside and was harnessed into a stone trough for thirsty travellers and horses.

Half way along Mill Lane was a small-holding called Alders where the Shaw then the Leiry family lived. They kept a cow and a few pigs but Mrs Leiry was best remembered for her hens that were constantly in danger of being run over by the Ashover Light Railway.

Walking along Mill Lane with the Amber Valley Camp on the right

The Amber Valley Campsite extended on each side of Mill Lane with a number of playing fields in the valley bottom and on the other side of the railway tracks. With the coming of the reservoir this area, the Mill and Mill Lane were totally submerged. To get an idea of where it ran, draw a visual line between the entrance to the Sailing Club and the North Bank Car Park.

4 WOOLLEY MILL

Drive into the North Bank car park opposite Hill Cottage on South Hill and you are on the opposite end of the original Mill Lane that led to Woolley Mill. It was situated in the dell at a junction where the River Amber changed its northerly course to flow westerly across the valley. From a very early date, the River Amber provided motive power for Mills all along its length and this mill at Woolley was built in 1640 on the instruction of Mr William Revell of Ogston Hall and is often referred to as Revell's Mill.

William Revell's estate, according to a fine levied in 1658 consisted of

'the manor of Ogston with appurtenances, 35 messuages (dwelling houses together with outbuildings, curtilage, and the adjacent land appropriate to its use), 20 cottages, 1 dove house, 1 water mill, 1,000 acres of land, 250 acres of meadow, 1,560 acres of pasture, 200 acres of wood, 1,500 acres of furze and heath and all manner of cattle'.

The mill was a two storey impressive stone building with a miller's house at the side and as the miller's working hours would be dictated by the river water which was hard to control, by placing the mill on a branch from the

Woolley Mill lies to the right of the photograph in the dip surrounded by trees

river, with a mill pond, the water could be regulated.

It was originally a Corn Mill constructed for the purpose of grinding wheat, oats and small amounts of barley for local farmers. It was advertised for sale in the Derbyshire Mercury in 1773, stating that it had three pairs of stones and a dressing machine for flour. John Wood is listed as corn-miller and farmer of Woolley, according to White's directory of 1857.

For a period around 1877, the mill lay disused but by 1899 it had changed usage and was being utilized to saw blocks of stone obtained from the local quarry. This stone was used to transform the frontage of Ogston Hall and provided more modest brick houses with stone window sills.

By 1912 Woolley Mill had again fallen into disuse and for many years it lay in neglect until it was finally demolished to make way for the reservoir.

5 RESERVOIR DAM

The cost of construction of an embankment or dam wall on the River Amber was estimated to be £400,000. Work commenced in June 1955, and it was hoped to have the construction of the embankment sufficiently advanced by October 1955 to enable about one hundred million gallons to be impounded.

The finished embankment was to be 65 ft high, 700 ft long at the crest and 355 ft wide at the base. The central trench below the dam wall and the wing trenches on the flanks were excavated down to the dense black shale underlying the site, and back-filled with concrete and puddle clay. The depth of the trenches varied between 55ft to 110ft.

The dam wall consists of quarried rock fill with a puddle clay core wall bonded by selected fill on either side. Grouting was carried out on the North and South sides to seal the underlying strata.

In October 1957, the embankment was 35ft high and the reservoir had risen to a height of 30 feet by December 1957. Two years later, the embankment was raised to its full height of 65ft and the overflow shaft, in plan having an internal diameter of 60 ft, was completed.

Messrs G.H. Hill and Sons (Manchester) were responsible for the design and construction of the embankment and the road diversions.

The dam wall

6 OGSTON HALL

Ogston is derived from the personal name Ogged and the Old English noun 'tun', meaning Ogged's farm. This name would have been allocated when the neighbouring settlements of Wessington, Morton, Stretton and Alfreton were founded, and these names were well established by the year 1,000 A.D.

At the time of the Domesday Book, Ogston was held by the Deincourt family. In the 14th century, it passed to the Revell family and remained with them until 1727 when the last male heir died. It then, through marriage became the seat of the Turbutt family whose continuous occupation lasted for

Ogston Hall was built in four stages and displays four very different styles of arcitecture from medieval to Victorian

246 years. As successors to the Revell family, the Turbutts sympathetically built up and improved the estate, reconstructing and enlarging the house.

The oldest surviving part of Ogston Hall probably dates from the mid-1550's when Robert Revell re-built the then existing small farm or manor house. A separate house was built by William Revell and his wife Mary, daughter of George Sitwell of Renishaw Hall in 1659. William Revell was the last of the Revells, and died in 1727

Mary Ann Revell, William's sister married Richard Turbutt in 1717. Through this alliance Richard Turbutt became possessed of a moiety of the Ogston estate. They had four children who all died in infancy and when Mary died in July 1724, Richard married Francis Babington with whom he had four children. Their only son William Turbutt married Elizabeth Burrow, daughter of the rector of Morton. Elizabeth's sister Mary married John Holland of Ford, so the two sisters became neighbours.

In 1767, to mark the beginning of a period of continuous occupation of the house and estate by the Turbutt family, the house was re-built to the east of the 1659 extension. The improvement in the estate during William's lifetime coincided with a period of economic prosperity. He was a typical example of a Georgian county squire and laid the foundation of Ogston as a county estate

Another period of prosperity was when Gladwin Turbutt married his first cousin Ellen Duppa Duppa and the young couple began planning the restoration and enlargement of Ogston between 1851-1854. The west wing was virtually rebuilt, the northern end made into a Brewhouse and the southern end into a new kitchen. The three individual houses were joined and excessive adornment and bay windows added. The work cost £3,077.13s. 5d. A new conservatory was built in the garden, then after the building work had been completed, plans were drawn up for a new garden layout.

Richard Babington Turbutt succeeded his father in 1932, but his time as squire covered the depression and the long period of lean years of the 30's when the return from agriculture was poor. To meet part of the liabilities of the death duties, 200 acres of estate were sold in Nov 1932. Amongst them was the Greyhound Inn at Higham plus land and farms at Mickley and Stretton.

A mortgage and the sale of a further 140 acres enabled the duty to be paid off over the next 10 years. By 1945, the estate had been reduced to 2,300 acres. Then compulsory measures were introduced that made it nor financially viable to own an estate, so in 1952 fifteen farms, forty houses and cottages, and 445 acres were sold, mainly on the eastern side of Ogston.

Finally in 1957–8, 225 acres of land on the north side of Ogston were acquired by the Chesterfield Rural District Council for the construction of the reservoir. This involved flooding the valley between Woolley and Ogston and the building of a dam between the spurs of land on which both Ogston and Ford House were situated, thus bringing a modern industrial plant to within several hundred yards of Ogston Hall.

In 1962 Richard Turbutt and his wife moved to Scotland and Ogston Hall was leased. In poor health, he returned to Ogston for Christmas 1963, and died on February 17th 1964 in the room where he had been born nearly 77 years earlier.

His son Gladwin put the Ogston Estate on the market in 1973. The Star Newspaper, Sheffield reported it as being a Medieval Mansion dating from 1002, with four reception rooms, fifteen bed and dressing rooms, and three bathrooms, in a 900 acre estate. It was offered for sale by auction by Strutt and Parker in the Midland Hotel, Derby on Thursday 28th June 1973 at 3pm, but two days prior, it was sold by private treaty to Mr Wakefield.

So ended a period of Ogston by the Revell/Turbutt family.

7 FORD HOUSE AND FORD OLD HOUSE

Ford House stood on a prominence of high ground across the river valley from Ogston Hall, overlooking one of the finest valleys in the country.

The loss was a double misfortune because not only was Ford House demolished, its predecessor known as 'Old Ford House' which was situated within its grounds suffered the same fate.

Ford is first mentioned in 1227 and by the latter part of the 16th century, the family of Curtis was established there as yeoman farmers.

Ford Old House

Ford Old House was probably built in the first half of the 17th century by Thomas Curtis. It was a charming stone house with a low roof of stone tiles, and small mullioned windows, facing south onto an open courtyard.

John Curtis sold Ford Old House to George Holland. It is believed that his son John, a successful maltster who made a modest fortune, extended the house on the Eastern side with a range of buildings believed to have been built as a malthouse. He also built a stable block across the other side of the courtyard.

His son and heir Thomas born in 1702 continued to expand his father's business as a maltster, and it is he who is credited with building a new house at Ford.

Ford House

The new house, a stylish Georgian building of elegant proportions was probably completed around 1725. It was built across the courtyard from the old house on the site of John Holland's stables and incorporated the old dwelling house which was turned into the kitchen wing of the new house.

Thomas Holland was High Sheriff of Derbyshire in 1763 and was later made a magistrate. His son John had a late marriage to Mary Burrows, daughter and co-heiress of the Rev Benjamin Burrow, Rector of Morton.

Mary's sister Elizabeth married William Turbutt of Ogston Hall so the two sisters became neighbours for many years, reigning over their respective households on either side of the valley.

When Mary died in 1847 at the age of ninety three, the estate was sold to Gladwin Turbutt of Ogston Hall and the two estates became one. In 1850, Ford House become the dower house for Ogston when Anne Turbutt lived there for five years. After that, it was occupied by a series of tenants, then sold for the last time in the 1950's to the Derwent Valley Water Board who were busy making plans for the new reservoir.

Although not within the reservoir area, it was considered that Ford House would be useful to the committee as a residence for staff employed on the proposed plant and the range of outbuildings could be used for stores. This proved impractical and the property lay empty for years; vandals took any item they could use or sell and by the summer of 1958 it was rubble.

All that now remains of Ford Old House and Ford House is the 17th century pigeon house and the walls of the 18th century kitchen garden.

8 ASHOVER LIGHT RAILWAY (ALR)

When the Overton estate at Ashover with 1,074 acres came up for sale in 1918, the Clay Cross company bought it for £33,075 in order to extract the natural resources. Fluorspar was used in the cast-iron foundries and the limestone ballast utilized in construction of roads and railways. To transport these resources to their works in Clay Cross, the Ashover Light Railway,(ALR) the last British narrow gauge line of any length was built. The route of seven and a quarter miles was roughly in the shape of an elongated letter S running from Egstow, Clay Cross to the Butts Quarry, Ashover.

The Jackson family had owned the Clay Cross Company since Robert Stephenson resigned in 1815. General Jackson was both creator and fond admirer of the Ashover Light Railway. The original four engines were bought at a cost of £1,000 from the War Disposals Board. All had previously seen service on the front line in France during the First World War. Later a fifth engine was added and they were all named after General Jackson's children Hummy, Guy, Joan, Peggy and Bridget. Construction of the line began in September 1922 and by January 14th, 1924 the railway was sufficiently complete to allow the working of the first goods train from Fallgate to Clay Cross. A short time later, General Jackson arranged a special train for his guests using cleaned goods wagons fitted with wooden seating, although Mr Thomas Hughes Jackson travelled in style seated in his own upholstered arm-chair. Fortunately, the weather was good.

The railway was officially opened on April 6th 1925 by Mr Thomas Hughes Jackson who, despite being in his ninety second year, drove an engine over

Joan pulling two carriages as she approached Ford

88

part of the route.

Although built by the Clay Cross Company for the transportation of natural resources, a directive from the Ministry of Transport ruled that the railway should also provide a full public passenger service to and from the isolated Ashover, so public services began the day after the official opening. During the second week of operations which fell at Easter, over 5,000 bookings were made.

Seven trains ran each day and served thirteen stations. From Egstow, Clay Cross, the line crossed the main A61 at Hilltop where the built up embankment still stands. It then veered south skirting Holmgate, through Springfield, over Clay Lane, then parallel to the main London, Midland and Scottish (LMS) Railway line through Stretton towards Higham.

Reaching its furthest point south, it then parted company as the LMS continued south to Derby and the ALR looped west to travel through the valley of the River Amber, proceeding through a gap in the low ridge between Ogston and Ford where the watercourse of the River Amber had to be diverted and straightened to eliminate the need to provide two bridges. The raised embankment running parallel to the Midland main line can still be seen.

Leaving Ford, the ALR was never far from the side of the river as they ran together, half hidden amongst the quiet woods and fields. This tranquil valley between Ford and Woolley Bridge was known as 'the bottoms', and passengers could alight at Hurst Bridge to enjoy a day in the heart of the country, picnicking and bathing in the River Amber.

Leaving Hurst Bridge on a rising gradient the railway continued along the

The Franklin family enjoying a picnic in pre-reservoir days

The Ashover Light Railway track through Dale Bank

Ashover Light Railway.

CHEAP DAY TRIPS TO & FROM THE COUNTRY

CHEAP RETURN TICKETS

WILL BE ISSUED ON

WEDNESDAYS, SATURDAYS and SUNDAYS,

As follows:—STATIONS AND FARES:

	Clay Cross	Chester-field Road	Holm-gate	Spring-field	Clay Lane	Stret-ton	Hurst Lane	Wool-ley	Dale Bank	Mill-Town	Fall-gate	Salter Lane	Ash-over
	d.	d.	d.	d.	d.	d.	d.	d.	d.	d.	d.	d.	d.
Clay Cross				3	3	4	7	8	8	8	10	10	10
Chesterfield Road						4	7	8	8	8	10	10	10
Holmgate						3	6	6	8	8	9	9	9
Springfield	3					3	6	6	8	8	9	9	9
Clay Lane	3					3	5	5	6	6	8	8	8
Stretton	4	4	3	3	3		3	4	4	4	6	6	6
Hurst Lane	7	7	6	6	5	3		3	3	3	3	5	5
Woolley	8	8	6	6	5	4	3		3	3	3	3	3
Dale Bank	8	8	8	8	6	4	3	3				3	3
Milltown	8	8	8	8	6	4	3	3				3	3
Fallgate	10	10	9	9	8	6	3	3					3
Salter Lane	10	10	9	9	8	6	5	3	3	3			
Ashover	10	10	9	9	8	6	5	3	3	3	3		

Children under Twelve years of age Half Fares.

The Tickets are issued on the trains, and by any train during the day; they apply to or from the Stations named, and are available for return on day of issue only

Trains leave Clay Cross, Week-days, at 7.20, 8.55, 10.33, 11.35 a.m. 2.35, 4.37 p.m.; Saturdays only, 9.25; Sundays at 7.40, 10.0 a.m. 2.30, 5.45 p.m.

Holmgate, Week-days at 7.28, 9.3, 10.43, 11.43 a.m. 2.43, 4.45, 6.30 p.m.; Saturdays, 9.33; Sundays at 7.48, 10.8 a.m., 2.38, 5.53 p.m.

Stretton, Week-days at 7.35, 9.38, 11.0 a.m. 12.2, 3.6, 4.52, 6.46 p.m.; Saturdays, 9.48; Sundays at 7.55, 10.18 a.m., 2.45, 6.0 p.m.

Ashover, Week-days at 6.70, 8.40, 10.20, 11.50 a.m.; 2.15, 4.0, 5.33, 7.30 p.m. Sundays at 6.40 a.m., 12.35, 4.40, 6.45 p.m.

Manager's Office, C'ay Cross, April 30/25.

JOHN MAY, Manager.

JOS. SPRIGGS, ALMA PRINTING WORKS, HOLMGATE ROAD, CLAY CROSS.

Day trip schedule

valley, crossing Mill Lane, the bridleway which led to Revell's Mill, skirted the playing fields of the Amber Valley Camp and proceeded to Woolley Bridge. This was the area where marshy ground had been encountered and during construction of the line, before the newly built embankment had consolidated sufficiently, the track had spread under the weight of the locomotive. Fortunately, the re-railing beams at each end prevented any serious damage.

From Woolley Bridge, the line continued through the quiet valley of Dale Bank. Milltown halt was only a quarter of a mile away and a favourite pastime was 'beat the train'. It was jokingly acknowledged that a passenger could leave the train, pick a bunch of wild flowers and still be in plenty of time to catch it at the next stops of Fallgate, Salter Lane and finally the Butts Quarry, Ashover.

Here, at Butts Quarry stood the 'Where the Rainbow Ends – Café', another brainchild of General Jackson who designed and named it after a play by Clifford Mills and John Ramsey. Built in wood to an unusual octagonal design and made by joiners at the Clay Cross Company, before being installed on site, the roof was covered by alternating courses of coloured roofing tiles in the colours of the rainbow.

The Rainbow Café as it was fondly called, not only provided refreshments for visitors during the day, it was also the romantic venue for Saturday night dances which for many ended in a shaky ride back to Clay Cross in the dimly lit carriages of the last train.

Unfortunately, the initial success of the ALR was short lived as the number of bookings taken in the first few weeks had stimulated the instigation of a regular bus service to Ashover. The number of railway passengers declined

The last passenger train on the Ashover Light Railway

gradually until eventually the daily passenger service became insufficient to pay even the conductor's wages.

Regular services ceased on October 3rd 1931 but passenger trains were still provided at holiday times although receipts continued to decline until the last scheduled passenger train ran on September 13th 1936. During this period, the Rainbow café's openings were restricted to weekends only during the summer months. But rather than lying dormant, between 1932-40, it was hired to the Derbyshire County Council as a domestic science classroom for the pupils of Ashover and Uppertown schools.

Passenger trains were still provided for special occasions like the 1937 Ashover Show and a garden fete at Ogston Hall in 1940, but the last teas were served at the Rainbow café in September 1939. With the outbreak of war, it was used as a school for evacuated children living at Amber House in Kelstedge.

The final passenger train of the Ashover Light Railway ran on Sunday August 26th 1947. It was a special for the Birmingham Locomotive Club.

Quarrying in Ashover closed in 1950 and the railway followed suit in March 1950. One diesel engine was retained to continue shunting operations at Fallgate Yard and this same engine made the final complete run on the line on October 23rd 1950 carrying Clay Cross Company staff who were assessing the land for sale.

The Rainbow café was dismantled and transported back to Egstow where it was reassembled on John Street, at the corner of the Clay Cross works playing field. Unfortunately, the distinctive rainbow tiles had been lost in transit, but in 1952, the Rainbow Cafe was re-opened in its new guise as a welfare and sports club for the Clay Cross company. It stood alongside a wooden carriage that had also served the route.

These two buildings were used for sport and recreational purposes for over fifty years, then in 2007 the site on which they stood was given planning permission for new development. The 'Where the Rainbow Ends Café' had to go.

In 1996, a small group of like-minded individuals with an interest in the Ashover Light Railway got together to establish the Ashover Light Railway Society (ALRS). The initial aim of the group was to record the surviving features and create a data base of known ALR artefacts. During 2001 when Ogston reservoir was reduced by 26% for repair work, the track bed of the ALR was uncovered and could once again be seen running along the valley of the River Amber. How this must have stirred the imagination of those members particularly when they found that the disused track bed of the ALR can still be traced at various places along the route and the 2½ miles between Dark Lane and Ashover Butts is surprisingly intact. This raised the question,

The Where The Rainbow Ends Café and one of the old carriages –
before being moved from Clay Cross

could the ALR be revived as a tourist attraction?

Imagine their delight when Maximus the owners of the Rainbow Café offered it to them. Would it be possible to move the building once again back to its original site at Ashover Butts? The restored building would be a key asset to the society providing a café for villagers and visitors, a useful source of revenue and an interpretation point for the ALR. The society received the blessing of the Parish Council; the owners of Ashover Butts supported the plan, but unfortunately finances were the major stumbling block. The cost of moving the café back to Ashover was estimated in the region of £100,000 and time was not on their side. The building had to be moved by September 2007.

It was thanks to a dedicated team of volunteers and a successful fund raising appeal that the dismantling and transporting was able to take place, and the sectional building is now in secure storage awaiting the next stage. Could this be the realisation of the societies main aim – to see narrow gauge steam trains running through the valley once more?

9 HIGHAM

The great Roman Rykneld Street ran straight through the centre of the linear settlement of Higham, the name meaning 'high homestead'. Roman coins found by Mr A Haslam in the stockyard of Well Farm at the north end of the village, might suggest there was originally a Roman settlement at this point, most probably the site of the Water Board.

Long after the Romans had departed, Rykneld Street continued to be a main highway and Higham's fortunes were linked to the passing trade which was sufficient to keep six inns in business along the 600 yard stretch of its main street.

In 1243, Higham was granted a charter to hold a weekly market around the market cross. This was also known as the butter cross because the farmer's wives sat on the seven steps selling their dairy produce. The cross, originally medieval was repaired in 1755 at a cost of 3s 6d (17·5p)

In addition to being the general hub of village life, the Black Bull Inn was the courthouse, and in the coaching era, an important staging post used by the 'Amity' and 'Telegraph' coaches until 1792 when the Alfreton-Higham turn-pike was opened.

Reputedly Dick Turpin stayed at The Black Bull Inn in Higham. Later it became Black Bull Farm and after a time when the farm was divided into several dwellings, one section was renamed Turpin Cottages. Locals also refer to the main road as Turpin Lane and according to legend, Dick Turpin's long

An early artist's impression of Higham

94

Higham as it is today

run can be accredited not only to luck but the fact that he had his horse shod backwards by a local smithy to confuse his pursuers.

The attractive stone cottages and farms of Higham had long been part of the Ogston estate, but after the war, local authority housing regulations required the improvement of many dwelling houses. Water closets had to be installed and houses brought up to certain minimum standard. In addition, the Ministry of Agriculture began to require certain improvements to farm buildings in order to conform to the new milk and dairy regulations.

Despite grants being given by the Chesterfield Rural District Council, the number of properties on the estate requiring modernisation meant that the outlay was considerable, and to make these improvements, the higher rents required from tenants would have been beyond their means. Tenants of the Ogston Estate had always been cushioned against the full rigours of normal housing costs, even if the standard of their housing was not of the highest.

The decision to sell the properties in Higham meant the end of the Ogston Estate as it had been built up carefully over the years. It followed many lean years, including the depression of the thirties, death duties, war years and for a decade after, the Government's policy of opencast coal extraction.

Some properties had been sold previously but in 1952, fifteen farms covering 445 acres and some forty cottages and houses in Higham were sold by Messrs J Else of Derby.

10 HIGHAM HILLSIDE

Leading from Higham down the hillside into the Amber Valley were old bridleways, one of which followed part of the present Ogston Lane crossing the River Amber by a bridge known as the Roman Bridge. As its name would suggest, tradition maintains that this bridge was built by the Romans.

Long before there were any settlements on the site, these bridleways formed part of a network used by the packhorse trains. With twenty of more animals carrying balanced loads of perhaps two and a half hundredweight on their backs, these packhorse trains regularly travelled the same set routes they had used for centuries. For isolated communities, the men who worked on those packhorse trains were a welcome source of news and gossip.

When the railways came to Derbyshire around 1836 to transport the vital elements of the industrial revolution – coal, ore, lead, limestone and fluorspar, the North Midland Railway Company acquired about thirty acres of Higham hillside from the Ogston Estate at an agreed price of around £3,000. The railway passes through a cutting immediately opposite Ogston Hall and a bridge was built to carry Ogston Lane over it.

Unfortunately, this also crossed part of the route of the medieval bridleway which led down to the Roman packhorse bridge over the River Amber, and having constructed a new bridge, the Roman Bridge was allowed to disintegrate.

Higham Hillside

The ancient paths led from Oxon to Trinity Chapel

A century later, the Government's policy of opencast coal extraction, started originally as a war-time measure, gave no consideration to the long term well-being of 300 acres of agricultural land on this hillside. Such wholesale disturbance of land couldn't fail to leave its mark, yet nature has now patched up the wounds and left us with only an echo of the past.

11 BRACKENFIELD

During the twelfth century, a new community between Wessington and Ogston appeared on an area of ground known during the 12-16th centuries as Brackenthwaite. It became known as Brackenfield and although the name points to Scandinavian origin and a much earlier settlement, there is no mention of it in the Domesday Book. This may be because the original settlers found the area too inhospitable and moved on.

This sleepy village can boast of having the largest village green in the county, and as part of their millennium celebrations, Brackenfield re-instated their old well on the Green.

Now, during the last week of May, well dressing takes place here. Well-dressing is the ancient art of decorating springs and wells with intricate pictures made out of petals, peppercorns, leaves and other natural things. It is a tradition that is unique to Derbyshire and the Peak District, and can be traced back to the old pagan custom of giving thanks to the water goddess.

*The Millenium Pump which draws water from the original well on Brackenfield Green.
In the background is the old village school, now the Parish Hall*

Admiring the work of one of Brackenfield's well dressings

98

The activity starts with the puddling of the clay to ensure the correct consistency, packing the pre-soaked frames with the clay for a good foundation to the well-dressing. The design is then sketched onto the surface followed by out-lining with peppercorns, wool, alder, cones, or straw. The design is then filled in with the appropriately coloured petals, leaves, wool, egg shells and other natural things. The process takes about 5-7 days to complete depending upon the size andcomplexity of the display. The results are stunning and well worth a visit during the construction and afterwards when the finished result, after being blessed in a church service, is left on show for several days.

Brackenfield well dressings are constructed in the Church Hall on the Green, the blessing is in the Parish church and displays are outside the school, the Methodist Chapel and Nether Farm, further down Church Street. For further details contact – 01629 534806.

11A & 11B TRINITY CHAPEL AND CHURCH

On the western boundary of the parish, high on the slopes of Highordish lies the ruins of the medieval Holy Trinity Chapel which is visited on *Walk 7*. Holy Trinity was a religious order founded in 1198, and it is believed that this medieval ruin is a rebuild of an even earlier building which may have dated

The ruins of Trinity Chapel

The ruins of Trinity Chapel

from then. There is a record from the 13th century of an ancient track named Chirchegate, meaning a lane leading to a church or chapel, which ran across the fields from Oxon to Holy Trinity.

Over the years, the attendance at this little chapel grew less as more conveniently positioned places of worship began to emerge for this scattered congregation. In bad weather, this out of the way chapel was often empty, but on Trinity Sunday, the Sunday after Whit Sunday, a carnival atmosphere prevailed and the church and surrounding hillside was packed with

Holy Trinity Church, Brackenfield

parishioners.

Although it had been suggested during the previous century, it was finally decided in 1856 to replace this chapel with the current Holy Trinity Church, just a short walk from the southern tip of Ogston Reservoir. The land was given by Mr Turbutt of Ogston Hall and his wife, Helen Turbutt, a very talented artist is responsible for painting one of the two stained glass windows on the south facing wall of the church.

Before it was abandoned, some of the fabric from the deserted chapel, including a chancel screen and two oak chairs were taken to the new church which was dedicated in 1859. A number of special events are being held in 2009 to celebrate its 150th anniversary, but the old Trinity Chapel is not forgotten entirely. Since 1913, an annual pilgrimage is held on Trinity Sunday. A procession forms on the Green and walks to the ruined chapel where prayers are said and hymns are sung at the site as they have been for eight hundred years.

12 OGSTON LODGE
AND THE GATEWAY TO OGSTON HALL

As the old Brackenfield to Woolley road had served the drive to Ogston Hall, when the road was changed, it was necessary to construct a new drive to the Hall nearer to Brackenfield to run along the southern edge of the reservoir.

The Lodge to Ogston Hall was also on the old Brackenfield Road and had

Brackenfield Lodge, now submerged under Ogston Reservoir.
Charlie Davies, the gamekeeper's son is at the gate

to be replaced by a new Lodge, immediately opposite the new drive entrance to the Hall. Brackenfield Lodge was designed and constructed by Mr M. Wheatcroft and built by Mr G.F. Sheldon on behalf of the Water Committee.

13 OGSTON NEW ROAD

At either end of Ogston New Road is a stretch of the old road from Brackenfield to Woolley, because the coming of the reservoir resulted in the submergence of a portion of this road making it necessary to construct a diversion to the west about a thousand yards long. It is carried across the tongue of the reservoir near Ogston Carr on an embankment.

The view from Brackenfield across the valley with the ribbon of road leading to Woolley. Most of this road had to be diverted for the reservoir. In the centre is the Amber Valley Camp

14 WOOLLEY AND WOOLLEY MOOR

Although not mentioned in the Domesday Book, Woolley has existed since Mediaeval times. Several theories exist as to the origin of the name. Some say it comes from the tufts of sheep's wool caught on the brambles, but historians say it comes from the Old English words 'wulf' – wolf and 'lea' – woodland or 'ley' – moor. This conjures up a picture of desolate countryside where wolves, bears and other forest creatures roamed freely.

Woolley and Woolley Moor have always been treated as two distinctly different areas separated by the River Amber. Until 1700, Woolley Moor was known as Moorwood and was part of North Wingfield parish, later Clay Cross. It included the hamlet of Fletcherhill, a few scattered farms and cottages, St Mark's Church/School, and Badger Hill, the area from the Toll Bar cottage to the White Horse Inn.

Except for the latter, this area has hardly changed, but during the 1950's the hamlet of Woolley Moor swelled with the ribbon development along the main road and the eighteen houses built to re-house the families who lost their homes through the building of the Ogston reservoir.

Woolley is the area west of the river, separated from Woolley Moor by the bridge over the River Amber. It is part of Brackenfield parish, originally part of Morton parish. It included a group of cottages on the main road, a scattering of cottages and the Methodist Chapel on Quarry Lane.

In 1938, Frank Bradley arranged for Dolman, Balfour and Beatty to supply electricity to Woolley, but most of the residents found this so expensive, they had shilling (5p) slot meters installed in order to pay. When the shilling ran out, the electricity supply cut off immediately without warning.

15 OGSTON BIRD CLUB

The Ogston Bird Club (previously Ogston Hide Group) was formed in the summer of 1969 and has become one of Derbyshire's premier bird watch sites. The club's objective is to build links between birds and those who are interested in their study and preservation. The stone 'hide', accessed through the car-park by the Sailing Club, was erected on June 20th 1969 on land rented from the Ogston estate and is open to the public. To date, 228 species of birds have been seen and recorded; some are rare like the Wilson's Phalarope, Sabines Gull, Ospreys and Long Tailed Skuas, and many breed within the area.

16 OGSTON SAILING CLUB

On January 4th 1960, a meeting was called for anyone interested in forming a sailing club on the newly formed Ogston Reservoir. For such a venture, the disused Amber Valley Camp was an ideal site complete with existing buildings.

Ogston was the first drinking water reservoir to allow sailing, but part of the original agreement was that all boats introduced to the site had to be decontaminated in a ceremony that was witnessed by the Water Authority at a cost of £3 per boat. In the beginning, the number of boats was limited to fifty with

Existing buildings were ideal for the continued use of Ogston Sailing Club

a membership of 100. In the 1970's the demand for membership rocketed and in the 80's sailboarding had an enthusiastic following.

During 2000/1 lottery funding was obtained to replace the old boat houses, buy training boats, and create a new race tower and jetty. Unfortunately this coinciding with Severn Trent's announcement that the reservoir would be drained to facilitate necessary repair work on the dam wall. The water returned in November 2002. The Ogston Sailing Club is affiliated to the Royal Yachting Association (RYA) and is an accredited RYA Training Centre.

Sailing boats on Ogston Reservoir

17 AMBER VALLEY CAMP

During the 1930's, the Government instigated a scheme providing a number of Camp Schools giving children from urban areas the benefit of a month's education in rural surroundings. The Amber Valley Camp at Woolley was one of thirty-one built by the National Camps Corporation of Victoria Street, London on a gently sloping, thirty acre site overlooking the beautiful open countryside of the Amber Valley. As one young scholar visiting in December stated –

The Amber Valley Camp School

Suffering a severe winter made the buildings resemble Swiss chalets

'The Camp was extremely attractive with its natural wood buildings and green shuttered windows, laid out round a grass quadrangle. Only a few more pine trees and steeper slope were needed to complete the illusion of a Swiss township of chalets with their little green balconies and wood tiled roofs. Knowing little of the difficulties of a severe winter, we admired the imagination of the National Camps Corporation.'

Set amongst lawns and flower bed, the buildings of cedar wood were designed with dormitories and classrooms heated by radiators and lit by electricity. There were water closets, showers, wash basins and baths with hot and cold running water, luxury indeed pre-war. The Assembly Hall was provided with a stage for dramatic work, and the kitchens were equipped

The large dining room at Amber Valley Camp

with the most up-to-date utensils and labour saving devices to serve the large dining hall.

With the building of the Amber Valley Camp, the local farmers were able to benefit from a telephone line taken into the area for the camps use. Prior to this, one of the few telephones in the district had been at the village post office situated by Woolley Bridge. Their number was Ashover 64.

DERBY SCHOOLBOYS EVACUATED TO WOOLLEY CAMP

When war was declared in 1939, it was considered a necessity to evacuate children from places thought to be at high risk from German air attack. One such area was Derby where the Rolls Royce factories and the railway workshops made a significant contribution to the war effort.

The headmaster of Derby Boys Grammar School, Mr Tom York secured the use of Overton Hall, and initially, one hundred and thirty boys from the school were brought from St Helen's House. But Overton Hall was not large enough to accommodate them all and some pupils were billeted to local farmhouses. One of those boys was the late Ted Moult, a T.V and radio personality whose career in farming could be traced back to the Overton experience.

Although the work of the lower school continued in safety far away from the anticipated targets, it was extremely difficult to run a school in two sections eighteen miles apart. Added to this, the first winter at Overton Hall was a hard one. Heavy falls of snow and high winds made the roads impassable and food and fuel had to be taken in on sledges. Overton Hall became the staging post for the eventual move to Amber Valley Camp where three hundred boys and masters could all be in one place.

Parents were given the opportunity to visit the camp on June 6th 1940. They were also provided with a leaflet with a photograph of the camp and details of its facilities. A further leaflet detailed the articles of clothing needed by each boy, not easy to acquire when a school uniform was compulsory and clothing coupons were strictly rationed.

Under the Government Evacuation Scheme, the arrangement for payment of maintenance fees was the same as for evacuation. No parent was required to pay more than 6/- a week for a boy, and those whose incomes were below a prescribed level were not required to make any payments.

For the boys at Overton Hall, the move to the Woolley Camp took place on June 24th 1940, and that September saw the whole school – three hundred boys and masters alight at Stretton station for the Autumn Term. Some of the masters were billeted to local houses. Mr Curtis and his family went to Ford House; the headmaster Mr Tom York, who was replaced in 1942 by Mr Leslie Bradley went to Handley House.

The school was once again in one location but under several roofs. There were four chalet type dormitories named after Derbyshire places – Eyam, Melandra, Cromford and Bakewell. Two similarly constructed buildings, Dovedale and Wingfield provided laboratory/classroom facilities and library accommodation respectively. A shortage of classrooms on the camp site resulted in lessons being taken at the local hostelry Napoleon's Home and at the Woolley Methodist Chapel, whilst weekly science lessons required the boys to be bussed to Tupton Hall School that had opened in 1936.

The Reverend A.G. Grime was resident house-master at the school and lived on the site with his wife Gladys and three daughters, Kitty, Chippy and Elisabeth. His door was always open to pupils in need of advice and to deal with the occasional bouts of homesickness. Some boys went AWOL only to be brought back by embarrassed parents the following day.

On Sunday there was the trek to Brackenfield church, and one of the few occasions when the boys from Derby would meet the boys from Hunstanton Prep School evacuated to Ogston Hall. The non-conformists or those who felt disinclined to walk the mile or so to Brackenfield attended the service at Woolley Methodist Chapel. There, on a cold winter's day, the congregation was either roasted by a coke-stove or gassed by the fumes.

The end of the war was greeted with mixed feelings as the whole school moved back to Derby. Elisabeth Bowden (nee Grime), the daughter of the resident housemaster who lived at the camp throughout the war, recalls how,

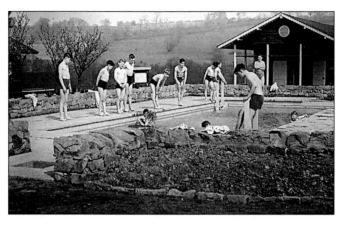

Recreational time for the boys at Amber Valley Camp

Boys at the camp helped with the war effort

at the age of nine, she cried when the war was over and they had to return to Derby.

> *'It was such a super spot,' she recalls, which is one reason why since organising a reunion on June 24ᵗʰ 1990 to mark the fifty year anniversary of the original occupation, the Derby School Reunions have became an annual event and a time to reminisce.*

Looking back, one of the old boys remembered a time when a lone German raider buzzed the camp.

'It is only in recent years,' he mused, 'I have pondered on the logic of evacuating children to an establishment that, from the air, must have very much resembled a military camp.'

Did the Amber Valley Camp resemble a military camp?

When the evacuated children left the camp in July 1945, it was retained by the Derbyshire County Council and under the headship of Mr John Gregory Morgan, the school reverted back to the purpose for which it was built. Children from surrounding towns had a term of schooling coupled with countryside pursuits at this idyllic rural retreat.

Then came the announcement that Ogston reservoir was to be built in the valley and although only the playing fields and a small part of the site was to be effected, a decision was made to close the entire camp.

Entertainment at Amber Valley Camp

The crowded dining hall at Amber Valley Camp

Evacuees camp now under water

JOAN 1992

ELISABETH Bowden, now of Bristol, believes this early 1941 photograph of Amber Valley Camp, Woolley Moor, may stir a few memories.

She says: "Derby School was evacuated to the camp in June 1940, for the duration of the Second World War.

"My father, the Rev A.G. Grime, was resident house master at the camp, and together with my sisters Kitty (now living in London), and 'Chippy' Irvine (now living in New York) spent a memorable six years in this lovely part of the country.

"Most of the area is now the Ogston Reservoir, and only two dormitories and the old dining room, now the Ogston Sailing Club room, remain.

● **Days of yore from 1941:** Derby schoolchildren evacuated to Amber Valley Camp

"On Sunday, June 24 1990 — 50 years to the day of the evacuation, I arranged a successful reunion of Derby School Boys...some had not met for over 45 years!"

"We decided to make this an annual event, and last year we assembled on Sunday, June 23. The second gathering proved just as successful, with some more new faces.

"This year, we met on Sunday, June 21, at the Ogston Sailing Club."

Plans are in already in hand for the 1993 gathering.

Contact Elisabeth at 17 Eastfield Road, Westbury-on-Trym, Bristol BS9 4AE for details.

'Evacuees camp now under water' – report in the Derby Telegraph newspaper

The stash at Amber Valley Camp that had been hidden for over sixty years

The engineer Mr P. Hothersall reported to the North East Derbyshire Joint Water Committee that – *'Having regard to the large number of occupants which the Amber Valley Camp accommodates, the continued existence of a camp alongside the reservoir would create some difficulty with regard to drainage and I would consider therefore that it would be advisable to acquire the whole camp.'*

Though the site was not submerged, the camp was closed, most of the huts were dismantled but the main dining block and two of the dormitory blocks remained.

When the Ogston sailing Club was founded in 1960, it took over the site. The two dormitory blocks were used for boat houses and the dining block became the Club House; but that's not the end of the story. After sixty odd years of continual use, the two old dormitory blocks were in a sad state of repair, so in 2001 a decision was made to demolish them. It was while they were being torn down that a horde of cigarette packets, empty 2d Smith's crisp packets, chocolate and toffee wrappers, a bag of liquorice allsorts, a comic, two newspapers and a letter dated 5.11.41 were found sandwiched between the outer and inner walls of Cromford dormitory. The letter was from a worried parent to her eleven-year-old son chastising him for smoking. The recipient of the letter, now in his late seventies and living in France can't recall concealing the stash that had been hidden for over sixty years.

18 WOOLLEY FARMERS

Reservoirs can only go in valleys and that usually floods productive and badly needed farmland, but it is generally agreed that a sheet of water can do much for the landscape.

Home after a hard day

The best arable land built on calcareous sandstone was down by the river, and much of the land covered by the reservoir was of agricultural value and distributed between the six farms along Hurst Lane, owned by Ogston Estates.

Marshalls who farmed Bottom Farm were worst affected, losing almost all of their eighty acres. Top Farm which had fifty seven acres was only slightly affected. Walnut Farm, Yew Tree Farm and Revel Farm each with fifty acres lost half their land. This was harsh because they were good dairy farms and not only did it restrict their farming, but the land that was left was mixed, which made farming much less economical. Mr Johnson of the Farmer's Union spoke on behalf of the farmers but to no avail.

19 LITTLE OGSTON OR OXON

The area bordered by the former course of the River Amber in the North and East and the Carr Brook in the South was an area known as Little Ogston. Within this manor lay the six previously mentioned farms, Top Farm, Walnut Farm, Yew Tree Farm, Grove Farm, Revel Farm and Bottom Farm. There was originally at least one more property in this group between Bottom Farm and Revel Farm in field OS2338, where only the old well can still be found.

Over the front door of Walnut Farm is a date stone 'WF 1764'. Coincidentally, these initials may stand for Walnut Farm or the tenant farmer at the time William Fidler. His burial entry on December 7th 1765 in Morton Church Register reads 'William Fidler of Oxon' which indicates that at that time, this farming community was known as 'Oxen' or Ogston.

These farms lie in a line along Hurst Lane, the old lane leading from Ford in the east, crossing the River Amber at Hurst Bridge then straight across the valley. The earlier name for this lane was Hengenedewey, meaning the sloping or overhanging way. Although the main part of Hurst Lane is under the reservoir, the site still exists at the car park, travels up past the entrance to the Sailing Club, branches with Quarry Lane and ends at Top Farm where it peters out into a series of footpaths. These are also ancient tracks that led to Trinity Chapel on the slopes above Mathers Grave.

With the disruption caused by the building of the reservoir, a reorganisation was needed but the only casualty was the sixteen acre Grove Farm situated in field OS0315 just at the point where the lane divides. According to a 1913 report, it probably dated from around 1545. In the 1880s it had its thatched roof replaced by a slate roof, possibly at the time when a number of freehold estates including those at Little Ogston were united in the Ogston Estate.

Yew Tree Farm was sold by auction without land and became a private house. Bottom Farm became a private house and the stone outbuildings are very attractive holiday lets, Top Farm and Walnut farm were combined, and the land was re-divided.

20 PRIMITIVE METHODIST CHAPEL

The Primitive Methodist Movement in Woolley began in March 1832 when fifteen residents met in each others homes and in the blacksmith's shop. Mr Job Bradley, a farmer residing at Brackenfield, was the leader, and for about half a century the name Bradley was honourably associated with Woolley society.

In 1840, a local farmer, Mr Elijah Draycott, gave them a corner of his field at a peppercorn rent, as the site for a little chapel with the seating capacity for one hundred people. It was built with stone from the nearby quarry under a pitched slate roof at a cost of £84. James Waine, a trustee and member of the society was the builder and left his initials JW carved over the entrance door.

James Croft, another trustee was the village carpenter and did the woodwork.

On a bend of Quarry Lane almost opposite the chapel was a short lane to Scotherns cottage. At one time, two families lived there.

Woolley Methodust Chapel prior to conversion

113

Local boys built stone huts in the quarry

21 DRAYCOTT'S HOLDINGS

Further along Quarry Lane was an old Yew tree and behind it Draycott's Holding, a property that had been in the same family for generations. It was listed as a farm shop, and sold pig-feed corn and flour. The men of the village used to congregate there, sitting on corn sacks to pass the time of day.

22 SHEFFIELD STREET

Making a cross-roads with Quarry Lane and the B6014 main road was Sheffield Street, a short lane on which there were six buildings. The only surviving building is Smithy Cottage. Next was Mr Ward's cottage, then Mr Booth's, then Mr Smedley's. What we would see as rustic charm was translated as unsanitary living conditions, and in less enlightened days, the council thought nothing of knocking these buildings down.

23 SMITHY COTTAGE

Smithy Cottage was originally two cottages. The first cottage was the home of Mr & Mrs Nichols who later moved to Scarborough. Next door lived Mr Young the Blacksmith and his wife Elsie. Mrs Nichols was the Young's daughter.

Mrs Young was affectionately known as 'Ma' Young as she had a tea shop much frequented by walkers and the boys of Amber Valley Camp. Once a term, the Trent Motor Traction put on several buses to transport fond parents, relatives and friends to Amber Valley Camp. A great treat for all on these occasions was a visit to 'Ma' Young's tea-rooms. Everyone tucked into cream teas and home-made cakes with beans on toast for the boys and boiled eggs for the parents. These were especially appreciated by the 'townies' limited to less than one egg per week on war rations. Some parents took the opportunity to stay longer and enjoy the Amber Valley, taking lodgings with local families.

Ma Young is recorded in Kellys 1941 directory as 'Mrs Elsie Young refreshment and rooms Woolley.' Her tea room is now the workshop of Smithy Cottage, but the present owner thinks it might have been a stocking factory some time earlier as the windows are very distinctive.

The Blacksmith's Shop, which stood on the right hand side at the end of the road fell into decay and was pulled down. There is now no evidence of its existence apart from the name.

24 DARK LANE

The stretch of the B6014, either side of Woolley Bridge is known as Dark Lane and between the Blacksmith's Smithy and Woolley bridge, the construction of Ogston reservoir required the destruction of a group of three buildings to the west of the river. The first was the blacksmith's forge that gave Smithy Cottage it's name, and another building that was occupied by Joe Sam the cobbler who was also the village postman.

Joe Sam would set off from Alfreton every morning with a bag of mail and walk to Woolley where he spent his day in a small hut mending shoes. Finishing work, he would pick up the return mail and walk back to Alfreton. He was probably his own best customer.

Lower down was the wheelwright's forge run, according to Whites directory of 1857 by William Fox and later by Joel Berrisford. Children used to watch the men hammering hoop wheels into circles to fit the wooden cart wheels. The metal hoops would be cooled in the nearby River Amber.

25 ASHOVER LIGHT RAILWAY CROSSING WOOLLEY BRIDGE

The application for a level crossing for the Ashover Light Railway to cross Woolley bridge was initially opposed by the Derbyshire County Council surveyor because he considered it a most dangerous place. He suggested an overbridge. The promoters objected claiming that this would cost at least £5,000 and his attitude was unreasonable.

In order to squash the objection, the Clay Cross Company carried out a traffic survey on Friday and Saturday January 24th and 25th 1919. These are the results :-

On Friday, between 7am and 7 p.m three motor cars and thirty six other vehicles passed the spot. On Saturday, market day in Chesterfield, two motor cars and forty three other vehicles were counted.

On this evidence, plans for the crossing went ahead, subject to the usual safeguards being provided, and between 1925-50, the Ashover Light Railway ran through the valley, crossing the River Amber and the B6014 road at Woolley Bridge.

This was one of only two gated crossings on the railway and for some years, the occupants of Amber House shared the task of opening and closing the gates with the train crew.

The station at Woolley Bridge with its short siding curved to follow the boundary wall of Napoleons Home orchard, was situated in a picturesque, though rather cramped location beside the River Amber. The siding terminated

ALR fireman Chrlie Maycock opens the gates for Bridget at Woolley Crossing 1943

The ALR track into Woolley Station showing the siding where coal was sold branching to the right. The stone wall on the right borders the orchard of Napoleon's home. The station platform is to the left with the River Amber behind the trees running almost parallel to the track. On the opposite side of the road is Amber House

at the Clay Cross company coal wharf and an office for coal sales, which closed in 1934, was manned by Charlie Biggin whose mother was housekeeper for Mr Hill at Oldfield House.

26 AMBER HOUSE / LAUNDRY COTTAGE

To the right of the railway line was Amber House, a picturesque rustic building built by Mr Kemp. Its bay windows and overhanging eaves were a feature employed in other buildings in the area. When Mr Pitts lived there from the 1920s-1940s, he was the official crossing keeper and had the responsibility of operating the crossing gates in return for free use of a small lineside allotment.

Later, when Amber House was occupied by the Towel family, the responsibility of operating the gates seemed to have lapsed and the train crew resorted to supplying a few choice lumps of coal, an effective way of relieving them from the chore.

Amber House was also known as Laundry Cottage. It acquired its name because all the laundry for the Sheffield Convalescent Home for men, based at Stubben Edge Hall from 1922 was done there.

Amber House with the dismantled ALR track in the foreground

Unfortunately, Amber House was one of the properties purchased by the Water Authority and inundated by the reservoir

27 FOX'S TRANSPORT

Harold Gerrard Fox is registered as Woolley Moor haulage contractor in Kellys 1941 directory. He had a lorry for, amongst other things, collecting the miner's coal entitlement from Oakerthorpe, and transporting the luggage of the boys from Amber Valley Camp to and from Stretton station. With the lorry piled high with luggage, the boys had to walk the one and a half miles which

Form 2B aboard Mr Fox's lorry

Mr Fox's lorry was used to carry all the luggage to the station

must have seemed an inordinately long way to the 'townies'. However, some boys managed to get a ride as this photograph of form 2B confirms.

The mass exodus at the end of each term was the occasion when bags and cases were stowed aboard the lorry, which was driven to the station followed by a long crocodile of boys on foot.

In 1923 H. G. Fox was registered as having two fourteen seater vehicles. One was a specially converted mail-van painted blue and called 'Blue Lady', or more derogatory, the flying hen pen. It had side seats and a half door at the back to take miners from Woolley to work in the Morton Coal Mine, and shoppers into Clay Cross. It ceased to operate after 1936 due to competition from East Midland Motor Services.

The other vehicle was a charabanc. When going on a journey up hill, someone had to sit at the side of the driver and prime a special attachment on the steering column which pumped petrol from the tank to the engine. As this was normally fed by gravity, it was either that or the vehicle had to operate in reverse. Once at the top of the hill, the charabanc came to a halt and everyone had to wait while the

Sitting on the bumper of the bus waiting for the engine to cool

The rear view of the Commer coach

WOOLLEY MOOR AND CLAY CROSS BUS SERVICE.

	MON.		WED.		FRIDAY							SATURDAY
	a.m.		a.m.	p.m.	p.m.	p.m.	p.m.	p.m.	p.m.	p.m	p.m.	
Woolley Moor (dep.)	11 30		11 30	6 40	2 35	5 20	6.40	2 25	5 20	8 0	10 10	
Handley	11 40		11 40	6 50	2 45	5 30	6 50	2 35	5 30	8 10	10 20	
Stretton Station	*11 45		*11 45	6 55	*2 50	5 35	6 55	*2 40	*5 35	8 15	10 25	
Clay Cross Victoria (arr.)	11 50		11 50	7 0	2 55	5 40	7 0	2 45	5 40	8 20	10 30	
			p.m.	p.m.								
Clay Cross (dep.)	12 20		12 20	9 45		5 50	7 10	2 50	5 50	8 30	10 40	
Stretton Station	*12 30		*12 30	9 55	Stops for work service.	6 0	7 20	*3 0	*6 0	8 40	10 50	
Handley	12 35		12 35	10 10		6 15	7 25	3 15	6 15	8 50	10 55	
Woolley Moor (arr.)	12 40		12 40	10 15		6 25	7 35	3 25	6 25	9 5	11 5	

No Service Tuesday   No Service Thursday

*Connects with L.M. & S Railway Trains at Stretton Station.

Proprietor,

H. G. FOX, WOOLLEY MOOR, STRETTON,
ALFRETON.

Jas. Springs & Sons, General Printers, Market Street, Clay Cross.

The time table

The old Commer coach was left to rot in a field

Getting the coach onto the recovery vehicle

engine cooled before the journey could continue.

These two vehicles were replaced a decade later with a new fourteen seater Commer coach with the registration number RB4757.

The service operated from Napoleons Home, Woolley Moor from March 1932.

Stoppard started a rival bus service to try to put Fox out of business, but they were unsuccessful and the service continued until just before Harold Foxs death on June 10th 1949.

The bus had no further use so it was put to rest in a field where in 1961, Geoff Lumb an enthusiast and collector discovered it rotting away. He

The newly revamped coach that had served the Woolley community for many years

wanted to buy it but Mr Edgar Fox, Harold's brother was unwilling to sell. Many years of neglect had resulted in broken windows, rotten panels, a decaying ash body frame and no rear wheels, but when Geoff returned in 1968 a sale was agreed. In the meantime, he had discovered that the 1932 Commer was very unusual.

Getting the bus onto the recovery vehicle was the first problem as the field was a honeycomb of rabbit warrens making it difficult to jack up the bus to re-fit the wheels which they found had been donated to another Commer vehicle.

Overall, the transformation took forty two years and the first outing after major restoration for the newly revamped coach was at the Nocturnal Rally in Huddersfield on October 26th 2003. It also returned to make a nostalgic visit to Woolley Show in August 2004.

28 NAPOLEON'S HOME

Almost directly opposite the junction of Badger Lane was the ancient hostelry, Napoleon's Home run by Mr Harold G. Fox who was also a wages clerk, parish clerk and manager of the school. As Mr Sam Fox, Harold's son said, you could free-wheel on your bike down Badger Lane and go straight in through the front door.

The three hundred year old alehouse was originally named the 'Travellers Rest' as it would have been a strategic point on the Mansfield/Matlock turnpike road and a stopping point where horses were changed and passengers refreshed themselves. The name may have been more apt than originally thought as this was a time when Inns and Ale Houses had no licensing hours and landlords had no power to turn out their customers. Many a traveller secured a cheap night's lodging simply by remaining all night.

It was some time around the beginning of the nineteenth century when the name was changed from The Travellers Rest to Napoleon's Home, and there is much speculation about this choice.

Could there be any connection between the French officers taken prisoner during the Napoleonic Wars and held in an open prison in Chesterfield? As they were allowed out on parole, they became quite well-known in the area. Some married local women and stayed after Napoleon's exile to Elba in 1814.

Or was it to even the score when an alehouse on Slack Hill, Ashover – demolished in the 1960s – was named The Lord Nelson Inn after Napoleon's arch rival?

The most widely accepted version appears to be that Mr George Elliot, the proprietor of the Travellers Rest at the time, went to France to fight in the Napoleonic Wars, and nicknamed Mark, his eldest son, Napoleon, so Mark's inheritance became Napoleon's Home and the name was retained.

Napoleon's Home, affectionately shortened to Nap's Home passed through marriage to the Fox family and the sign above the door in this photograph

Napoleon's Home

123

says:-

NAPOLEON'S HOME HAROLD. G.
FOX, LICENSED VICTUALLER
RETAILER OF BEER, WINE &
FORTIFIED SPIRITS TO BE CONSUMED
ON THE PREMISES. DEALER IN
TOBACCO

Nap's Home had a well in the
grounds and as the water supply for
the people in the Smithy Cottage area
regularly dried up, they used it too.

The hand operated village petrol
pump was situated by the side of
Nap's Home, in front of a stone barn
that housed four cows and a horse.
This is where Mr Harold Fox parked
his coach and where the service to
Clay Cross ran from.

Inside Nap's Home, the bar was
boarded off from the kitchen. There
was a staircase up to a large club-
room and during the war when the
Derby grammar school were at
Amber Valley Camp, extra classroom
facilities were provided here. This
was also where dances were held, but

Nap's Home with the village petrol pump situated outside the stone barn

according to Mr Sam Fox, they had to stop because the floor used to bounce and a great bulge appeared in the back wall.

With the decision to build the reservoir, the days of the old coaching inn were numbered and although not inundated, the site of Naps Home was considered too close to the water line for safety.

29 WOOLLEY HOUSE HYDRO

Woolley House, originally a large country house built by John Bradley, later become Woolley Hydropathic Establishment. Hydrotherapy is a remedial water treatment used in baths, douches, steam and hot air. Recognised as a medicinal therapy as far back as the Romans and Greeks, it was developed in 15th century France and 200 years later used in England as an adjunct to other methods of medicinal treatment especially in the control of high fever. It was frequently recommended for patients suffering from muscular weaknesses, stiff joints, and certain skin disorders.

Fashionable spa towns grew up where a mineral spring, known as a spa bubbled up to the surface and 'taking the waters' became a popular diversion during the nineteenth century. Physician, found the waters efficacious for almost every ill of the human body and although anyone could indulge, to enjoy the full treatment one had to be fairly well off as the Hydropathic establishments, or Hydros for short, were really luxury hotels that utilised the spa waters and made a lot of money for their owners. Hydros were run along

Woolley House

125

the lines of our present day Health Farms.

If the spa water was warmer than normal, had gases present or was heavily mineralised, it was considered eminently suitable. To possess all three qualities was a sure winner.

The Ashover area is rich in old lead mines and the water which accumulates in the mines is pumped up and discharged into a drain or outlet channel called a sough. It is a known fact that although some hydros were fed by springs others acquired their water from soughs where the water was warm. There is at least one local swimming pool that was, and still is, fed by sough water from which the steam can be seen rising on a cold day.

It may be a coincidence but water was pumped from the Gregory Lead Mine at Milltown and fed into a sough to be ejected into the River Amber at Woolley Moor, so Woolley Hydro could have utilised this sough water for their treatment. Cockle sough still ejects water via a low drain into Ogston.

With improvements in medicine at the beginning of last century, the hydros began to decline. During the First World War, many hydros were commandeered for the use of the military as hospitals and after the war they closed never to re-open. Woolley hydro was no exception.

It was sold and divided to form homes for 6-8 families. Attached to it was a small village shop and post office run by Mrs Anne West and accessed down an internal passage. Her brother-in-law Joe Spencer had a paraffin round and lived at Perkin's Cottage, Badger Lane where he too had a shop. Parlour shops like these seemed to be able to supply everything from a box of matches to a hundredweight of corn.

In the yard at the back of Woolley House was the old joiners shop which was also used by the local undertaker.

30 OLDFIELD HOUSE / NEW NAPOLEON

Oldfield House was built around the beginning of the twentieth century by John Bradley who also owned Woolley House/Hydro. The building at the back, recently converted to a separate dwelling and now called Oldfield Barn was the wash–house where the laundry from Woolley hydro was done.

When the hydro was sold, John Bradley retired to Oldfield House where he had running water installed in three of the bedrooms; luxury indeed at a time when most of his neighbours were collecting their water from wells.

In the late 1950's, the licence was transferred from Napoleon's Home to Oldfield House which became a public house called The New Napoleon. Fifty years later it was converted back into a private house and has resumed the name Oldfield House.

31 THE WHITE HORSE INN

The White Horse Inn on Badger Lane which is also known as White Horse Lane, is an old coaching inn built in the 1700's. It was once common practice for commercial buildings to display signs for those unable to read and inn signs have a long history. The sign here depicts a horse and cart carrying a 'badger' of salt, an old name for a measure of salt – thus the name 'Badger Lane'

32 WOOLLEY SHOW & WOMENS INSTITUTE

In June 1911, after King George V. Coronation celebrations in the village, 13s.10d (68p) was left over, and someone suggested putting it towards a village show. The first meeting was called on July 28th 1911 and it was decided to call it 'The Woolley Moor Vegetable Society'. It was to be open to members living in Handley, Woolley and Woolley Moor, and the first show was held on September 2nd. 1911, in Mr Mycock's field on Temperance Hill where stalls were set out under the damson trees.

Six years later, in 1917 the ladies of Woolley and Handley joined together to form one of the first Women's Institutes in the county. No early records have survived, but in 1920 and for many year after, the W.I. ladies provided refreshments at the Woolley Show.

The original 1911 Show Committee

The show grew and in 1923 moved to the football field adjoining Napoleon's Home where it was held for thirty five years. The last show there was in August 1958 as the valley was filling with water, then it moved to a new site by the side of the New Napoleon. More recently it has moved to the Jubilee Recreation Ground in Woolley Moor.

The show has changed over the years but the aim is still the same – to offer a day of entertainment for the village and provide keen competition among the gardeners of the district.

Sadly the Handley & Woolley Women's Institute hasn't flourished quite so well. In April 2007, the ladies celebrated their ninetieth birthday, but with dwindling numbers the nine surviving members made the decision to close. Their final meeting was held on November 15th 2007.

33 TOLL BAR COTTAGE

All along the turnpike roads were positioned toll-bar cottages to collect the tolls paid by people using the road. This in turn paid for the maintenance of the roads and was better than the earlier system when each parish had been responsible for the repair of its own roads.

This cottage at the junction of Ashover New Road and Badger Lane would collect the toll on the turnpike road which ran from Tupton to Dark Lane Woolley Bridge.

A new and more direct route, the B6036 New Road opened in October 1872 reducing the distance from Stretton station to Ashover by a quarter of a mile although it was still a three and a half mile journey.

34 BADGER LANE

Badger Lane is now the name of the road that runs between the end of Stubben Edge Lane and down to Woolley Bridge, the old turnpike road that carried passengers and goods. The name derives from 'badger' meaning a measure of salt.

Originally however, it was the name of the small hamlet consisting of five dwellings between the Toll Bar Cottage and the White Horse Inn. It was renamed Woolley Moor when extended with new building after the war, then expanded still further with the extra eighteen houses and bungalows built to re-house the people who had lost their homes due to the creation of the reservoir.

35 THE NETTLE

According to the story of how this delightful country pub got its name, in the early 1700s a merchant seaman who skippered a ship named 'The Nettle' became the new landlord and named it after his ship.

Another version says how a previous landlord was a keen greyhound courser who called his best dog Nettle. The dog went on to win the prestigious Waterloo cup so to commemorate the occasion, he renamed the inn. Sadly, after checking with the Coursing Club, I found this is untrue. No dog named Nettle has ever won the Waterloo Cup although many bitches of that name have sired dogs that have.

The name has been changed several times since then, but always around the same theme. It has been 'The Nettle', 'The Greyhound' and 'The Well Run Nettle'.

In the 1820s, one of the rooms at The Nettle was used as a courtroom for Mr William Milnes, a local magistrate who lived at nearby Stubben Edge Hall.

Members of the Barlow Hunt meet regularly at The Nettle Inn

36 EASTWOOD HALL

Eastwood Hall, originally known as Newhall, is now an ivy clad ruin on the outskirts of Ashover. It was in the possession of Serlo de Pleasley who died in 1203, passed by marriage to Isidore Reresby 1282 and remained in the Reresby family for 340 years.

Sir Thomas Reresby spent £2,000 on rebuilding the Hall in 1600. Until then it had no doubt been a farmhouse. Sir Thomas was a gambler and in order to

The ruins of Eastwood Hall

pay off his debts and afford a dowry for his three daughters, he mortgaged the property to Sir Samuel Tyron, who subsequently repossessed. He sold it to the Rev. Emmanuel Bourne in 1623 for £510. (equivalent today of £150,000). Sir Samuel Tyron was Emmanuel Bourne's patron.

During the Civil War in the1640s, when the Cavaliers and the Roundheads were bent on destruction, the Rev. Emmanuel Bourne and his wife Jemima made up their minds not to take either side.

Several times Eastwood Hall was plundered of goods and books that had taken more than twenty years to collect and the house was barbarously torn apart. Both sides were responsible and due to this, The Rev. Emmanuel

Jemima and Emmanuel Bourne

Bourne laid aside his surplice and prayer book and even stopped praying for the King in public.

During this time, all church marriages were banned by the Parliamentarians, and any couple wishing to marry did so in front of a Justice of the Peace in a brief wedding ceremony intended to be based on simple purist lines. The magistrate and registrar who conducted such ceremonies locally, was John Spateman who lived at Roadnook, Brackenfield.

When the Kings cause became hopeless Emmanuel Bourne accepted the appointment of Commissioner of Sequestration, thinking that by doing so, he could soften some of the hard measures dealt out to the Kings friends, but unfortunately this made him very unpopular.

Despite everything, Eastwood Hall was destroyed in June 1646 by the Roundheads. Leonard Wheatcroft, the church clerk at the time composed this doggerel:-

> *The Roundheads came down upon Eastwood Old Hall*
> *And they tried it with mattock and tried it with ball*
> *And they tore up the leadwork and splintered the wood*
> *But as firmly as ever the battlements stood*
> *Till a barrel of powder at last did the thing*
> *And then they sang psalms for the fall of the King*

It is thanks to Rev. Emmanuel Bourne that inside Ashover church is one of only twenty one lead fonts in England. The base dates from 1886 but the upper part of stone covered with lead, ornamented with twenty upright figures is considered to be Norman from around 1150. It was saved from being melted down for Civil War bullets by Rev. Bourne who buried it in the kitchen garden at Eastwood Hall.

37 STUBBEN EDGE HALL

The area of Stubben and the people who dwelt at the Hall have a long, interesting history. Early reference from August 15th 1319 records Ralph de Reresby of Eastwood Hall selling 'the land where hermits formerly dwelled' to Godfrey del Stubbynges. This name could have been derived from the practice of clearing the wolf infested forests, uprooting trees and 'stubbing' the forests. The family of Stubbynge survived there until the 15th century and were replaced by the Criche family. When Richard Dakeyne married the widow of William Criche, he inherited the property. After she died, he remarried Catherine Strange, daughter of the Earl of Rothes. She was the

Stubben Edge Hall

favourite maid of honour of Mary Queen of Scots and attended her unfortunate mistress to the scaffold.

The house passed through marriage to the Hopkinsons and others until in 1820 it became the property of William Milnes, the local Justice of the Peace who held court at the nearby ale-house. At this stage, the house would have been little more than a farmhouse until in 1821, William Milnes, using stone from the local quarries at Alton and Ashover, built the two storey Georgian style mansion, incorporating the modernised and improved 17th century core.

In 1873 Sir William Jackson purchased Stubben Edge Hall from Frederick Arkwright. Sir William was an original director of the Clay Cross Company with George Stephenson who had founded the company in 1837 after discovering coal and iron while excavating the mile long railway tunnel which passes under Clay Cross and emerges on Higham Hillside.

At that time Clay Cross was a small farming community, but George Stephenson provided houses for his workpeople, schools, chapels and in 1851, the church of St Bartholomew. At the outset, the company concentrated on developing the collieries and can take credit in being the first ever to send a consignment of coal by rail to London.

Stubben Edge Hall became the home of Sir William's son John Peter Jackson, Managing Director of the Clay Cross Company from 1876-1899. John Jackson's wife Florence instigated the formation of the Ashover Women's Institute on February 6th 1917. Until it folded in 2003, this was one of the oldest W.I's in the country. Woolley was formed the same year and has just

celebrated 90 years, but sadly due to decreasing numbers that too has now closed.

Mrs Florence Jackson, as the widow of Sir John Peter Jackson, had the honour of driving the inaugural Ashover Light Railway train over part of the track on April 6th 1925.

The Stubben Edge Estate with 717 acres was sold in August 1921 to Sheffield Works Convalescent Association which was officially opened by The Duke of Devonshire in July 1922.

In 1962 it was purchased by Major David Kenning whose grandfather started the Kenning Motor Group in Clay Cross, and in April 1984 it was sold to Granwood Holdings and remains the headquarters of the company.

38 ASHOVER

Ashover, which is often described as a 'romantic and picturesque village set in a deep valley surrounded by trees', could be called Woolley Moor's larger neighbour. In 2005, against stiff opposition from forty other villages throughout England, Ashover had the honour of being awarded the top prize in the Calor Village of the Year competition.

The name Ashover comes from Saxon times as 'Essovre', means 'Beyond the Ash Trees', so it is not surprising to find that Ashover was mentioned in the 1086 Domesday Book.

Ashover Parish Church was erected between 1350-1419 incorporating some earlier stonework. Stone heads of Edward 1 and Queen Eleanor are either side of the main entrance, but at the apex is Margery Reresby of Eastwood Hall. Not the usual practice of a loyal subject, but after all she did donated the doorway in 1275. Inside the church is a Norman font dating from 1150 and made of stone covered in lead. It is extremely rare and only one of a handful in the country. Rather surprisingly, the third bell of the eight is dedicated to the Emperor Napoleon because its predecessor cracked while ringing the news of the abdication of the French Emperor following his retreat in 1814.

There are three very popular pubs in Ashover; The Poet's Corner, The Crispin and The Black Swan. Named after the Patron saint of Cobblers and saddle makers, the Crispin was once a cobbler's shop. Alternatively, it could have been named in recognition of the Battle of Agincourt fought on St Crispin's day October 25th in 1415 as a thanks for the safe return of the Ashover men that fought in the battle and returned unscathed. The Crispin also took a prominent part in the Civil War when the Royalists troops turned out the landlord and drank all the ale. The Old Poet's Corner was previously the Red Lion and now attracts real ale enthusiasts from a wide area.

The Black Swan was regularly featured in the TV series 'Peak Practice'. It's over 300 years old and the sport of Bear Baiting is said to have taken place in a large hollow above the Black Swan. The Basset Rooms previously the Parish Rooms, is an impressive mullioned building built as a girl's school in 1877. The redoubtable inscription 'Train up the child in the way he should go and when he is old he will not depart from it' over the door emphasises the strong moral stance of Victorian educational principles. With the introduction of free state education in the late 19th century, this school was no longer needed so the building was converted to the Parish Rooms. It was recently changed to the Bassett rooms in recognition of the work of a benefactor of the parish.

In its present form, Ashover Agricultural and Horticultural Show can be traced back to 1924 when it was decided to resurrect the agricultural events that had taken the form of smaller shows and ploughing matches as far back as 1880. The first show held in the Rectory Fields took place on September 16th 1925 with an admission charge of 1/- (5p). Entry charges have increased but the show on the second Wednesday in August is still held in the Rectory Fields. It has continued to grow and now attracts a crowd of 15,000.

Ashover in the 1930's looking towads the Red Lion, now the Old Poet's Corner